Wicca
for
Couples

Making Magick Together

By

A.J. Drew

NEW PAGE BOOKS
A division of The Career Press, Inc.
Franklin Lakes, NJ

WICCA FOR COUPLES
Typeset by Eileen Dow Munson
Cover design by Cheryl Cohan Finbow
Printed in the U.S.A. by Book-mart Press

To order this title, please call toll-free 1-800-CAREER-1 (NJ and Canada: 201-848-0310) to order using VISA or MasterCard, or for further information on books from Career Press.

The Career Press, Inc., 3 Tice Road, PO Box 687,
Franklin Lakes, NJ 07417
www.careerpress.com
www.newpagebooks.com

Library of Congress Cataloging-in-Publication Data

Drew, A. J.
  Wicca for couples : making magick together / by A.J. Drew.
    p. cm.
  Includes bibliographical references and index.
  ISBN 1-56414-620-0 (pbk.)
    1. Witchcraft. 2. Love—Miscellanea. I. Title.

BF1572.L6 D74 2002
299—dc21

                                                        2002071920

"The books all talked about love and nature. I didn't see anything wrong with that."

—Denessa Smith, as quoted by
The Detroit News, March 7, 2001

For Tempest Smith

You left this world with so much
left unsaid.

Acknowledgments

Before anyone else, I must acknowledge my young friend Hanna Sowers, because in her spirit, I see hope. Next, I must acknowledge two people who certainly gave me hope. My dentist, Dr. Speer, and his assistant Nikki Marchetti. In pain, writing this would have been impossible. I was absolutely terrified of medical personnel, especially dentists, but with their very kind and warm approach to medicine, I was able to mostly sleep through a no-gas root canal. I am sure some of that kindness tempered a few of the rants found here.

Tempering some of those rants as well is Mike Lewis at New Page Books who, in his role as initial editor, treated my last manuscript with the same warmth and kindness as did Nikki and Dr. Speer treat my dental work. With his sense of humor, I have been able to take constructive criticism a bit better. Oh, editors still bug me a bit, but you have to laugh when someone tells you that you're sounding like "Attila the Wiccan" again. Also at New Page, I have to give thanks to Laurie Kelly for letting friendship survive poor communication.

Still on the issue of tempering, but perhaps on a different side of the fence, I must acknowledge Lisa Braun at Llewellyn Worldwide for demonstrating that there is at least one bright star visible in every storm. If I survive this one, I hope one day to return the favor.

Without Dorothy Morrison (sexy in red) who publicly declared me the "Prince of Yetis" in her book *Enchantments of the Heart*, this book would not have been possible, because it was from that very book that I drew the confidence to continue my search for the "Princess of Yetis."

Without Patricia Telesco (the All Godmother) to point me in the direction of my first book sale, there wouldn't be a second, much less this third.

Without M.R. Sellars (murder mystery author supreme), I wouldn't have opened my eyes to the tremendous value of the genre in which he writes. With those eyes closed, I surely would have missed one of the most important issues addressed herein. For without the work of fiction that is the story of Romeo and Juliet, I would never have spotted the very real union of Gavin Bone and Janet Farrar as example for Chapter 2.

Without Sirona Knight's teasingly playful approach to sexuality presented in her book *Love, Sex, and Magick*, I might have thought the issue of sex was still off limits in the Pagan community.

Most importantly, I acknowledge my readers: the great many good folk who have purchased and recommended my books so often that my editors let me get away with just a little bit more with each new book. Thanks to you more than anyone else. I may not be the most famous Witch in the United States, but with your support I am certainly well on my way to becoming the world's most infamous. I pray that I do not disappoint you with this book, and thank each and every one of you for giving me the career that I now enjoy. For you, I say, let us begin with:

"Cry 'Havoc,' and let slip the dogs of war"
—William Shakespeare, *Julius Caesar* 3.1

Contents

Preface

On the morning of February 20, 2001, a young woman named Tempest Smith woke, showered, and ate a bowl of Frosted Flakes as she did many other mornings. After breakfast, she put on her makeup, leaned into her bedroom mirror, and kissed her reflection. We know this because the lipstick marks were still on her mirror when her mother found her lifeless body. After kissing herself good-bye, Tempest tied a scarf around her neck and hung herself from her own bunkbed. Tempest was 12 years old.

Tempest's suicide wasn't yet another case of a Pagan crying persecution for the sake of attention. The trials and tribulations of her day-to-day existence and the reasons for taking her own life were written clearly in her journal. She was oppressed for being different and tormented by her peers for being Wiccan. She took her life because she could take no more abuse. When asked about Tempest's involvement in Wicca, her mother, Denessa Smith, said, "The books all talked about love and nature. I didn't see anything wrong with that" (*The Detroit News*, March 7, 2001).

When the news of Tempest's death hit the Pagan community, rage turned into a desire to place blame. Some blamed her mother for not seeing the warning signs. From what I understand, there were no warning signs. Others blamed the school, but if that blame is deserved, better it be placed by the courts. I blamed myself. Lots of people dream of writing books, many have the talent, but only a very few are fortunate enough to be published. Truth be told, it is more of luck than anything else that authors are published. I am one of those very rare and lucky people to whom the gods granted this fortune. They gave me a voice that can reach more people than I can number, yet I wrote nothing that would have changed Tempest's mind had she read one of my books.

I already had been working on this book for a couple of years when I first learned of Tempest's story. Hoping that I might be able to say something that would make a difference for the other Tempest Smiths of the world, I put this book on hold so I could work on one for pre- and young teens. I survived my own experience as a Pagan in the public school system because I had the multidenominational and unconditional support of my family. Specific religious affiliations didn't matter much to my parents as long as I remembered that "God is Love." I hoped to share that with our young folk, to show them that *family* is a very important part of our "family religion," even when that family is not Wiccan. My agent sent my proposal off to a major publisher. Part of their letter of decline reads:

> "...we do feel that in order to have a wide appeal, a book for teens on the subject would have to take a darker, more sophisticated tone."

I suppose the importance of family and love are not dark or sophisticated enough for that publisher. Has your heart ever been trapped between laughter and rage? Unfortunately, much of what I'd suspected about Wicca's relationship with the publishing business was confirmed. Even with my Leo pride, I was not happy to be proven right. The letter only got worse.

My motto had become: "Wicca is not a fashion statement." To this, they subtly replied that if I yielded my opinion, they might be interested:

> "...the author would have to be open to the idea of teens experimenting with Wicca for fashion's sake..."

In all fairness, the publisher did make it clear that they consider Wicca a "legitimate religion" and did not want to publish anything that is "potentially harmful." For the most part, Tempest's mother was right. Most books on Wicca do *talk* about love. Of the closeness between coven members, Raymond Buckland wrote: "In fact, the members of your coven frequently become closer to you than the members of your own family, hence the Craft is often referred to as a 'family religion'." (*Buckland's Complete Book of Witchcraft*, lesson 5). Mr. Buckland is not alone in his teachings. Because so many of today's books on Wicca express similar opinions, the trend of our "family religion" is to be set apart from the family. To the enrichment of Corporate America, that trend has been very profitable. Profitable because it seems the nature of youth is to rebel, sometimes even from those who love them.

Wicca has become big business. For the most part, big business doesn't care about Tempest Smith or anyone else who turns to Wicca as a valid spiritual path. What they usually find is that the corporate offerings are little more than fashion statements with none of the "love" that their books speak of. And authors have lined up to feed Corporate America exactly what they want.

"Would you like fries with that McWicca?"

The problem does not rest in what books on Wicca are saying, but rather in what they are *not* saying. Although it might not be correct behavior for friends and family members to scorn you for your religious choices, it does happen. And without a support structure, you will be ill-prepared for that scorn. We are a social creature. We desperately need the love and support that family and friends provide. Covens may seem to offer that love and support, but unless they are built on the same sense of love and communal interdependence that is the structure of family and friendships, then they just don't work.

Tempest's mother said that the books on Wicca all talk about "love"; Raymond Buckland said Wicca is a "family religion"; publishers tell us that they do not want to produce anything that is "potentially harmful." If religion is the path on which we find God and "God is love," how is it that books on our "legitimate religion" are more focused on casting spells than forming relationships?

Can't anyone see the harm in producing books that promise family and love, but that contain no real instruction on finding or building either?

For Tempest Smith, and for all the Tempest Smiths of the world, young and old, male and female—here is my apology, here is my heart, and here is my solemn pledge: If this book should alienate me from publishers and destroy my career as an author, then so be it. If this book should be the banishment of my good name from the Pagan community, then so be it. If that be the case, I will have no more love for the Pagan community than that which Tempest received from its empty words.

But in so doing, I will do so in accordance with the Wiccan Rede, which, in part, instructs: "Never a season with a fool shall ye spend"—because only a fool does not offer reciprocity unto love.

Introduction

Where be these enemies? Capulet, Montague,
See what a scourge is laid upon your hate,
That heaven finds means
to kill your joys with love;
And I, for winking at your discords, too,
Have lost a brace of kinship. All are punished.

—William Shakespeare, *Romeo and Juliet* 5:3

If you have read the story of Romeo and Juliet without shedding a tear or the movement of your heart, then you are not worthy of having read that great work. If you read this book without shedding a tear or the movement of your heart, then I am not worthy of having written it. As was the story of Romeo and Juliet something that had to be told, so is this view of Wicca one that must be told. If here I fail to do it justice, I welcome the humbling of the next who would do so.

In my first book, *Wicca for Men,* and then again in my second book, *Wicca Spellcraft for Men*, I started with a quote from *Macbeth* by William Shakespeare and explained that the Bard knew very little about Witchcraft. Here I quote *Romeo and Juliet* because that same man did know a great deal of love. What, some might ask, does Witchcraft have to do with love? Within the pages of this book, I hope to give you that question's answer.

The Pagan movement that we now enjoy is not an entirely novel idea. There have been many attempts to rebirth the old religions. Each of those attempts failed because they did not meet the needs of its members. If our new or Neo-Pagan movement is to avoid a similar fate, it must seriously reconsider its place in the lives of its members. Nowhere is this more important than in the relationships that we form. Nowhere is this more clear than in the Neo-Pagan religion Wicca.

The Wiccan community can be seen as two almost entirely different communities that share a common name. On one side of the fence, we have members who have taken the idea of an eclectic religion so far that calling them Wiccan is a tremendous stretch of the word. These are the fashion-statement Wiccans.

Fortunately, these people are easy to avoid because they are readily identified by their excessive use of black (both for clothing and makeup), their frequent visits to chiropractors to repair the spinal damage that was caused by the weight of huge pentagrams worn around their necks, and most importantly, their insistence that their fashion statements are religious in nature. I call that sect of the Wiccan community the *Rubs* because they rub me the wrong way.

On the other side of the fence, we have mature and sincere members who have examined their relationship with the world and have decided that Wicca is a sensible approach to further that relationship. These folk are both new to Wicca and long-time members. They are solitary practitioners and coven members. They are traditionalists and eclectics. And yes, some of them wear more black than the night itself, but their use is fashion for fashion's sake. They are the people who make Wicca a religion. I call these people the *Lifers,* because unlike the Rubs, the Lifers make Wicca a part of each and every moment of their lives.

When I started research for this book, I thought the Lifers mostly ignored the Rubs, poking fun at them only on occasion. I thought the Rubs responded by seeing Lifers as Wiccan dictators. But then I discovered something very interesting. I remembered when I was myself a Rub. Back during those days, we were called "Wanna-bes." Remembering that, I came to respect the Rubs just a little bit more. You see, it is impossible to be something without first wanting to be it.

This book is for the Lifers and those who are still balanced on the fence between the two sides of Wicca. This book is not for the Rubs. However, I do not say this out of disrespect but out of need. Back when I first discovered the movement, I was first rejected time and time again for being a Wanna-be, a Rub, or whatever you want to call it. Fortunately, I met a few who saw through my adolescent games and allowed my heart to grow Wiccan. But what about those who are not as fortunate? Isn't it the heartfelt duty of those who are fortunate, to want to share that blessing with those who are not?

So if you think that dressing funny and annoying your neighbors is a part of the Wiccan religion, then please read something else. However, if you find Wicca in your heart, then please continue to read my desperate plea that we stop our bickering, unite as family, and show these folk the way to our hearts. After all, it does take a village to raise a child and although they might seem incorrigible and even delinquent at times, weren't we all?

Something very real is happening in our religion, something so profound that if we give it a chance, Wicca may very well fulfill the promises that it has made. However, if we do not give it the attention that it deserves, we will miss the opportunity to bring Wicca into its rightful place as the beautiful religion that it is.

That profound event is that Wiccans are growing up. Sure, the teen fad continues, but many of those teens have matured and now realize that you simply cannot find a deep personal relationship in a cardboard box. Perhaps more importantly, some of the smaller publishers are starting to figure this out as well. Gradually, we are seeing more and more books that focus on spirituality rather than spells. The Wiccan community is still divided in its nature, so it is divided in its demands, but a handful of publishers have started to recognize the demand for sensible literature. Like all fads, the one that has swept the Wiccan community will pass. The huge publishers who pushed pop Wicca to the masses will move on to the next fad and the publishers who provided sensible literature will continue to serve the Wiccan community well.

This era is our turning point, not just for the Wiccan community, but for the whole of our world. We are poised at what may well be the beginning of World War III. It might also be the time in which the warring clans that threaten world peace realize they have more commonalties than differences, more love than hate. It is the time when we must do far more than walk the walk and talk the talk. If Wicca truly sees our Lord manifested in everything masculine and our Lady manifested in everything feminine, then we must see our Creator manifested in every union of the masculine and feminine and all things that spring from those unions. Not just on our altars, but also in our rites, and most importantly, not only within our own small community. We must demonstrate that reverence for life in a way that others will follow.

It is important to point out that this view is not homophobic. We are all composites of the masculine (God) and the feminine (Goddess) principles of the universe. Whenever we interact with others, that interaction is between the masculine and feminine principles of our souls. To say that this is not the case in a same-sex couple would be to put the format of a ritual before the meaning of the ritual. For the purposes of this book, when I refer to a couple as a male and a female, I am referring to the many male/female interactions that take place between a couple, and not the act of coitus that is symbolized in every Wiccan rite.

"...for behold, all acts of love and pleasure are My rituals."

—From the Charge of the Goddess
Author deliberately not cited (see Chapter 2)

Yes, it is hard to understand the many interactions of male and female. The Wiccan religion uses them as models of the Creator because they are how we create life. But no one with any sense can say that humans are capable of understanding the whole of creation. Instead, religion is a method of understanding the world in which we live in a manner that makes sense to our far less than perfect human minds. All religions accomplish this in one of two ways: They either treat the Creator as a complete mystery or they create a system in which we can understand the incredibly complicated universe in much less complicated ways. Wiccans use the latter, because we seek a personal relationship with the Divine and it is difficult to form a deep personal relationship with someone who is a complete mystery.

Part of making the incredibly complex universe easier to understand is making its Creator easier to understand. To this end, Wicca views the Creator of life in the way that we create life, as the union of male and female. We only run into a problem when we confuse this vision with sexual preference and the actual, physical creation of children. As I demonstrated in *Wicca Spellcraft for Men*, being male has very little to do with what it says on your driver's license. Our Lord and Lady are alive in each and every one of us. Gay, straight, black, white, male, female, or somewhere in between. This is also true of Christians, Muslims, Jews, and the whole of humanity, as well as its many paths. Each understanding the same Creator in a way that is hopefully best suited to their understanding.

Thus, the many religious wars do not find root in conflicting ideas of religion, but in the attempt by one person or group to force these methods of understanding on another person or group. This is the objectification of our Creator. It is the act of causing the Creator to be immutable and unchanging. Such an act destroys the personal relationship that can be had with the Creator, because it focuses a religion on a thing rather than a relationship. It is the act of making "what" more important than "why." This is why religions often fail their followers. This is akin to a marriage that fails because it was built on the looks of a couple (objectification) rather than the interactions (relationship) between its members.

For the furthering of a loving relationship, it is not the individual that we should focus on; it is the interaction between individuals. To further our relationship with the Creator, it is neither on the Lord nor the Lady that we should focus. Instead, it is on their interactions with each other. Because Wicca teaches that the Creator is immanent (internal) as well as eminent (external), our religion offers a level of intimacy that is not available in other religions. Our relationships with all things external are our relationships with our Lord and Lady. Nowhere is this relationship more direct than in our relations of the heart. For every time a Wiccan makes love, he or she does so with his or her Creator.

That is where every Wiccan couple must focus if they are to receive the rewards that our religion offers: not necessarily in the physical representation of making love (sex) but in the real Great Rite of making love. This is not the act of bringing the athame to the chalice that earns the title "symbolic Great Rite." It is the interaction between the chalice (feminine) and athame (masculine) that matters. As every human is a complex intermingling of both masculine and feminine, it is not the act of bringing the penis to the vagina that earns the name "Great Right"; it is the union itself. This interaction, this relationship, is at the very heart of our religion. Because Wiccans see our Lord in every man and our Lady in every woman, the act of sexual union is the act of touching our Creator in the most intimate way.

Thou art God.

Thou art Goddess.

In this respect, we are not all that different from more dominant religions. The symbolic Great Rite can be compared to the Catholic rite of receiving Holy Communion. Where Catholics symbolically eat of their Savior's body and drink of His blood, our symbolic Great Rite serves as a symbolic communion with our partner (Savior). Each is a symbolic act in which the Savior joins with our body. In the case of the Catholics, He symbolically joins at the belly. In the case of Wicca, he or she joins at the very root of our driving force to create. But just as Catholics use the symbolism of eating of their Savior's flesh and drinking of His blood to represent union, Wiccans do not view the actual act of sex as union. Even the actual Great Rite is not the rite itself. Instead, the Great Rite itself is only symbolic of the real union being honored. That union is of the heart.

Yes, I did say Savior. When we consider the lives of the pre-Christian country-dweller on which we often claim our religion is based, we find the nature of Wiccan salvation. You see, living off the land was not the easy life that many have romanticized it to be. Without family, your chances of survival were bleak. Children were a blessing of more than just heart. They were also a blessing of necessity. A new child meant there would soon be a new person to plant, harvest, gather, hunt, and defend the tribe. Children were salvation and each person carried only half of what was necessary to create one, so the bearer of the other half was a savior. Today, children do not play that essential role in our survival, but few can argue that life is not much easier when you are in a loving relationship. As many will point out, being loved is salvation from the darkest part of our souls.

Consider the word *religion*—"re-legion" or "re-join"—and you can see that Wicca does not differ from other religions in its attempt to unite with the Creator. Earlier I compared the Great Rite to the Catholic rite of Holy Communion. I'll take that comparison one step further before I contrast the two. Catholic lore tells its members that humanity became separated from the Creator and that only via communion with their Savior can they find their way back to grace. Wiccan lore also teaches that we are separated from the Creator. You see, although every man is God and every woman is Goddess, it is only the union of God and Goddess that is the Creator.

The first real difference in these two forms of Holy Communion is not in the format of the rite, but in the meaning associated behind that rite. Our religion is nature-based, so where other religions seek re-legion with a supernatural being in the sky, Wiccans seek union with the Creator in a much more natural way. We seek to unite with the very real and natural representations of our Lord and Lady right here on Earth. The second and much more important difference is that the Christian Savior is no longer in this world as flesh and blood. Although they can partake in a symbolic communion, they cannot have supper with him. Our saviors are right here in this world. Although we can partake in a symbolic communion (the symbolic Great Rite), we can also partake of the Great Rite (making love) and experience first hand the true union with our own personal saviors.

This key difference between Wicca and other religions is why it is possible for wars to go on without end. It is why children can be sent into shopping malls to detonate bombs. It is why airplanes can be used as missiles against innocent civilians. It is why governments can machine gun students for having objectionable ideas. This key difference between Wicca and many larger world religions is that Wicca teaches that the victims of those tragedies are themselves sacred. When an arm is found in the carnage of the aftermath, that arm belongs to our Creator! Our hearts sink because that arm belonged to someone we have a deep personal relationship with: our Creator. Thus, from a Wiccan perspective, crimes against humanity (indeed crimes against all earthly things) are crimes against the Creator.

So what happened to us? We have this incredible structure for a religion that can strengthen the bonds between us and the ones we love, while all along keeping in kinship with the Earth and guiding humanity towards a better world. We have a religion that values the relationships that form between people so much that the most holy of acts is one that can bring couples closer than any other. But instead of using our religion to unite us with the ones we love, we run around looking for covens of people whom we do not know, or declare that we are solitary practitioners and then conduct ourselves as isolationists. Do these sound like the actions of a fertility religion?

What has happened is we have lost our focus. We have forgotten what a fertility religion is all about. We followed people whose intent might come into question after reading their claims. In a recent book, one of the leaders whom we had looked up to for years proclaimed that she is "one of the most famous Witches in the United States today." Well Ms. Most Famous Witch, Richard Nixon was one of the most famous presidents in the United States. Being famous is not always a good thing.

A religion that is based on furthering unions is not nearly the same headline material that black cloaks and semisecret ceremonies are. As a result, the media has swarmed around those nut cases who practically scream, "Look at me I am Wiccan," when the real story goes unheard. This creates a public demand that money-hungry Corporate America is quick to exploit. Presto, chango: We have a religion that has been sterilized, sanitized, and placed in a cardboard box. When this happens, Wicca looses its meaning. It becomes bland and becomes unable to offer the rewards of a fertility religion.

In this book, I will demonstrate three things:

1. First (Chapter 1), the foundation of any religion is law. Wicca is no exception. While it may seem that Wicca has no rules, the very nature of our religion insists that we have no choice but to follow the law, because this law is in our very nature, and because that very law is in and of itself love.

2. Second (Chapter 2), that our fertility religion has been all but sterilized by the industry that has grown up around it. Our law has been all but omitted because it simply does not fit into a cardboard box. It cannot be marketed, forced, or sold. So the industry that has propelled Wicca these many years has simply left it out.

3. Third (all remaining chapters), that we can return fertility to our fertility religion, and love to our law.

So, if your soul screams for something more than religion in a box, then here is my attempt not to soothe your soul, but to point it in the direction of soothing. For a book cannot content your desire, but knowing others share the same desire just might.

The Foundation of Our Fertility Religion: Love— It's Not Just a Good Idea, It's the Law!

1

Do what you like so long as you harm no one.
—From *The Meaning of Witchcraft* (1959)
by Gerald B. Gardner

Introduction

Hey, wait a minute. What's going on here? That's not the right quote. It goes more like this;

"An it harm none, do what ye will."
—From the Rede of the Wiccae
by Adriana Porter[1]

Or maybe it goes more like this;

"An ye harm none, do as ye will."
—From the Wiccan Rede,
Author unknown

It seems that the more you read, the more inconsistencies you find. Consider the many origins of the Wiccan Rede. Some people claim it is ancient, but didn't find its way into print until 1975. Others say it was written by Gerald Gardner, Doreen Valiente, Lady Gwen Thompson, Adriana Porter, or Sybil Leek.

I have read that ancient European Pagans made dolls out of cornhusks. I have read that the ancient Celts once formed potato cults. I have also read that both cornhusks and potatoes were New World discoveries, which were not available to either the ancient Europeans or the Celts.

For each of these instances, I could read on and on, but in the end, what it always boils down to is the simple fact that just being in print does not make it correct. Instead, read what you will, listen to what you will, watch what you will, and talk to whom you will, but let common sense tell you when an information source is giving an accurate account, has strayed into fantasy, or has simply run amuck.

Case in Point:

During the late 1970s and 80s, a rash of women popped up on the television talk-show circuit. They had a common story, insisting that they were former Satanists who had borne children, and then sacrificed and ate those children. From woman to woman, the story varied a little, but in each, common sense forced a reasonable person to ask why these women had not been arrested for their criminal acts. The answer is that the acts did not take place. Instead of being seeded in reality, the stories were the result of false memory syndrome. It turns out the women did share a practice, but it was not Satanism. No. Instead, the commonality was the school of psychology, which used hypnosis and drugs to fabricate their memories rather than uncover them. The matters of supposed Satanic abuse of children were investigated by the FBI and dismissed (per "Investigator's Guide to Allegations of 'Ritual' Child Abuse" by Kenneth V. Lanning, FBI Supervisory Special Agent; January 1992).

Ultimately, you decide what you will believe. Just ask yourself which source your common sense tells you to believe.

Because there is so much contradicting information available about the ancient fertility religions, this chapter has been written more of common sense than of research. Here I have combined much of what I have read with what I consider common sense. The result is that I have relied on what I see as constants. In those constants, I see many things that are true today that must also have been true to the ancients. No matter what is written now or what was written then, the Earth is and was round. I believe that an equally true constant is that we are a social creature, dependant on family, friends, and community for our very survival. For me, that is common sense.

Have you ever felt alone? Not alone in the moment, but completely and utterly alone? Have you ever found yourself in a place so dark that death seemed preferable to the empty feeling in your soul? If you have, congratulations on your survival. Some aren't nearly as fortunate as you and I. The others had no idea what they were capable of overcoming.

There was a time when I thought our God and Goddess had forsaken me. I'd fallen very ill and feared I would not recover. Rather than continue a life of pain, I crawled to the comfort of my favorite shotgun. I put the barrel in my mouth and put my finger on the trigger.

"O happy dagger,
This is thy sheath. There rust, and let me die."
—William Shakespeare, *Romeo and Juliet* 5.3

Someone stopped me. Before I tell you who she was, let me first tell you that I hadn't slept in days. I was taking prescription steroids, which definitely alter mood if not mind. I was constantly oxygen-deprived due to the medical condition that I battled (sarcoidosis). With that said, I'll tell you she was that whom I'd always felt estranged from. She was Goddess herself, and in her presence, I was God.

The best way to sum up the experience is to say that I saw her for just an instant, but in that single moment when she appeared, I received the answer to every mystery. A moment later, I had forgotten all but the smallest bit of wisdom. What remained of her message was something I already knew:

"Ye must live and let to live"
—From the Wiccan Rede

It had been hiding from me in plain site. I had called myself Wiccan for many years and Pagan for even more years, but the secret, the mystery, the very core of our approach to life had escaped me. It wasn't just the words that made the difference, but the knowledge that someone could love me so much that she would give herself to me at the very moment that I needed her.

I had been in that dark place because, until that moment of my salvation, Wicca had failed me in much the same way as it had failed Tempest Smith. I left that dark place because the universe reminded me of a very important fact: that I am divinely loved. As a result, I sold my extensive gun collection; used the money to open a Pagan shop; became a vegetarian; and eventually became an author hoping to share that moment with the world and maybe in the process, find my goddess manifested in one of her Earthly representatives. All because I once felt more alone than any living creature should.

Although you might not think that feeling could protect one against a hostile world, it is humanity's greatest strength. It drives us toward union with others. It has been humanity's primary saving grace. Compared to other creatures of this world, we do not jump high, run fast, or hide well. If not for our overwhelming drive towards uniting with others, we would have become extinct long ago. It has been our greatest driving force.

The Law

Addressing this force has been the very function of religion (re-legion). It is why ancient religious law has set forth rules affecting matters of marriage, raising children, and social conduct. Some of these laws have withered with time, others remain pertinent to our times. I am sure you can see how the law of Moses, which forbids murder (unjust killing), is a good one to keep on the books. On the other hand, there is a Norse law that instructs its followers to always bring a sword to the outhouse. Some of these ancient laws do seem ridiculous in our modern world, but that does not mean we give up on the principle of law. Where would the world be if murder were an acceptable way of settling a dispute?

These laws are the very foundation of a religion. They declare that which the religion is: a path to re-legion, re-joining, and re-union with the Creator.

So just who is this Creator? Well, that question has turned to argument so many times that it is probably one of the single largest causes of war. It is certainly at the root of most of the problems that currently threaten the global community. The answer is difficult, because the fact is, we simply do not know. How then, in all of our ignorance, has virtually every religion come up with one of the same laws?

Buddhist: Hurt not others in ways that you would find hurtful.

Confucian: Do not unto others what you would not have them do unto you.

Christian: All things whatsoever ye would that men should do to you, do ye even so to them.

Hindu: This is the sum of duty; do naught unto others which if done to thee would cause thee pain.

Islamic: No one of you is a believer until he desires for his brother that which he desires for himself.

Jain: In happiness and suffering, in joy and grief, we should regard all creatures as we regard our own self.

Jewish: Whatever thou hatest thyself, that do not to another.

Sikh: As thou deemest thyself, so deem others.

Taoist: Regard your neighbour's gain as your own gain, and your neighbour's loss as your own loss.

Zoroastrian: That nature alone is good which refrains from doing unto another whatsoever is not good for itself.

So common is this law, that it is even found in secular teachings where religion is often not found:

The Golden Rule:
"Treat others as you want to be treated."

(Author unknown)

This common religious law exists because the prophets of these religions did not see the Creator as entirely separate from ourselves. What one does to others, one does to the Creator, because each and every one of us is part of the Creator.

This is expressed in common Wiccan greetings:

"Thou art God" and "Thou art Goddess."

It is only in the loss of this concept that some of these religions have found themselves at odds with each other. Only the insane would kill another for the Creator when the victim his or her self is the creator.

In Wicca, that law is the Wiccan Rede. It is *our* foundation. In its shortest version, it says, "An ye harm none, do as ye will." No one really can be sure who first wrote it. Certainly it is similar to what Gardner said in his book *The Meaning of Witchcraft* (1959):

"Do what you like so long as you harm no one."

Although it is an unpopular belief, I think the contemporary origins of the Wiccan Rede can be found in Aleister Crowley's Law of Thelema: "Do what thou wilt shall be the whole of the Law".[2] It is easy to see how the Law of Thelema could seem like a free-for-all when taken out of context. However, this is also the case with the Wiccan Rede.

In the case of the Law of Thelema, Aleister Crowley expanded upon the simple line often quoted as the Law of Thelema, saying that "Love is the Law."

Think on that for just a moment; "Love IS the Law." That is the force that we have been unable to fully define during the vast number of years humanity has walked this Earth. That unyielding force IS the law. Well, of course it is. After all, isn't it love that brings man to woman, Lady to Lord, God to Goddess, thus bringing forth all that is?

Love is the fifth Element, it is our spirit, the force that brings the other four Elements to each other. For ultimately neither God nor Goddess is Creator. Instead, it is their union that is the Creator, and that union is love.

In monotheistic terms: "God is Love."

In wider terms: "The Creator is Love."

Oh my! Mom and Dad were right!

Even if we do not recognize the connection between the Wiccan Rede and the Law of Thelema, the principle that "Love is the Law" can be supported elsewhere in Wiccan lore.

One of the few things that all Wiccans seem to agree on is that our religion is either based on ancient Pagan fertility religions or is itself a descendant of those same religions. Some choose to believe it is a postmodern revival of those religions in a modern context. Others choose to believe it was itself a pre-Christian fertility religion that hid from the church during the times of oppression but remained intact over those many hundreds of years. Chances are, it's a little of both. Some practices have survived more or less intact since before the Church State's rule.

Consider the Olympic Games. Once outlawed by the church, their clearly Pagan ceremonies are now seen across the world on our postmodern television sets. Consider the Christmas tree, which many of today's Christian churches forbid due to its Pagan origins. Then there is my favorite example: the maypole, which was once outlawed by the Church State.

But dancing the maypole, decorating a Christmas tree, and watching the Olympics does not make one a Pagan, much less a Wiccan. Although each of these may have been conducted as parts of ancient Pagan fertility religions, it is in the why of these practices that we find our seemingly contemporary law in ancient fertility religions.

Life before fast food, grocery stores, and automobiles was not as it is presented in the majority of modern literature. Life expectancy was low, infant mortality rate was high, and there was no shortage of suffering. For an idea of just how hard life was, we can look to Roman records, as the Romans were very fond of discovering such information by census.

Estimates during the Roman Empire:

➢ Life expectancy at birth was 25 years.

➢ For every 1,000 babies born, 319 were still births.

➢ Live births per mother averaged 5 per woman.[3]

These statistics mean that most mothers could look forward to birthing six or seven children, one or two of which would never take a breath. She would then die before she was little more than a child herself.

In Egypt, matters were worse. Almost every Wiccan has a working knowledge of Isis, the Egyptian Great Mother. What many do not know is that during the height of her worship, Egyptian mothers generally died between the ages of 23 and 25. This is hard to imagine when we live in a culture where being younger than 25 is cause to be banned from some public offices, as well as a few nightclubs. By today's standards, Isis would have had trouble getting good automobile insurance rates.

The rest of their lives are equally hard to imagine. It is from the adversities of these hard-to-imagine lives that something beautiful can be seen—our law. Men and women did not come together out of fancy. Children weren't born simply because there was no knowledge of birth control. These things happened because they had to happen. These things happened because we were born to love and that love is what has kept the human race alive these many years. The beauty in these ancient fertility religions was that although it might not have been written yet, the law was demonstrated in the actions of the ancients.

To understand this principle, one must understand evolution. Giraffes survive because their long necks allow them to reach the leaves on which they feast. This does not mean the giraffe grew its neck long to reach those leaves. It means they did not perish because their necks were long. Humanity did not learn to love because it was necessary for our survival. We did not perish because we have love. The giraffe's neck is long because the giraffe has no choice in the matter. We love because we have no choice in the matter.

Let's call it *communal interdependence*. Women risked death to bare children because those children were needed. The children were born because "Love is the Law." You see, that law is not only of man, but of nature. It is the law of survival. Even with the invention of artificial insemination, it is only in union that we are able survive. The beauty in the ancient fertility religions is that they recognized this aspect of humanity. Today we praise independence. The ancient fertility religions, however, demonstrated their concern for the relationships between people rather than the independence of any one person.

We tend to talk a lot about the God of the Hunt and the Goddess of the Harvest. But if not for one's children or the children of others, who would farm and hunt? Male children quickly joined the ranks of male labor and female children quickly joined the ranks of female labor. In the case of the female workforce, I did not intend a pun when I used the word labor. While birthing children was definitely a necessity, so were many other tasks. So, adults were dependant upon children; children were dependant upon adults; women were dependant upon men; and, yes, men were dependant upon women. That is where the foundation of the ancient fertility religions can be found, not in the want, but in the need. Not in the action (the what), but in the law (the why). We have survived because we love and because that love causes us to unite against forces that we are otherwise ill-prepared to face.

Of course, there are many forms of love that do not lead to childbirth. But at the root of it all are the unions that produce offspring. After all, I cannot love you like a brother if I have not been born, now can I?

➤➤

So what of that maypole dance? It was banned for many years because it was a symbol of that communal interdependence. It was a celebration of the union between men and women. The maypole is a clear phallic symbol and weaving of the ribbons around it symbolized the entry of the penis into the vagina. It was a form of the symbolic Great Rite. It is no coincidence that traditionally young men and women intertwined during the dance. It is the symbol of the intertwining of all things male and female in our lives, a celebration of sacred union, and the marking of what is now our law—love. With that in mind, it isn't much of a leap to see the phallus represented in the Christmas tree. Of the Olympics, well they were reportedly banned because they were conducted in the nude, and it does seem that ever since the Adam and Eve story the Christian church has always connected nudity with sin.

But even in our revival of the ancient fertility religions, much of our law remains lost. Think of everything you have read about the Horned God and how his primary job was to ensure a good hunt. Why then, I wonder, were Kernunnos, Pan, and Hern often depicted with an erect phallus? They were depicted with erections because without the union of Lord and Lady, male and female, there would be no animals to hunt and no one to hunt them. While some might not feel as I do, that animals other than humanity have the capacity to love, they certainly demonstrate an adherence to the law. Without love, there would be nothing. It is truly our greatest strength. It saved me from death at my own hand.

Our Greatest Weakness

> "Tis better to have loved and lost
> Than never to have loved at all."
>
> —Lord Tennyson

Love is also our greatest weakness. It is what caused Tempest to die by her own hand. You see, Lord Tennyson was right. It is "better to have loved and lost than never to have loved," because even having not loved, we are born with its desire. The Wiccan community lost one of its greatest leaders in Tempest, a person who loved so deeply that with no love from her peers, she preferred death. I can tell you this because I was there, too.

I urge her mother to publisher Tempest's journal. I here pledge any effort I can offer toward accomplishing that task, asking only that any profit gained be given to an organization worthy of Tempest's memory.

Without that work to cite, we have the story of Romeo and Juliet. In their story, we see love change from a great strength that would unite warring families into a great weakness that gave both families sorrow. In this case, the transformation was caused by collapsing avenues of communication.

Most often it is the case that love is our greatest weakness because we choose to welcome those who should not be welcomed, befriend those who should not be befriended, and ultimately trust those who should not be trusted. When those confidences are betrayed, we often find ourselves in an even darker place. I can tell you this because I was once in that dark place myself.

So how do we decide who should be given our deepest trust and who should be set apart from our heart where they can do no harm? How could we have told Tempest that the peers who tormented her should have been placed outside of her heart, where they could not have caused her death?

Here, too, is the function of religious law. If a mother loves her child, surely that love will cause her to defend her child. If one loves his family, surely one will protect that family.

Here is where our law is most often misunderstood. The eight words of the Wiccan Rede that are most often quoted do not instruct that one should not cause harm. Instead, those words tell us to take a desirous action should it cause no harm but does not in anyway tell us what to do should an action cause harm. How could anyone think that the law of a fertility religion could forbid the protection of its children?

While it is easy to think that we should allow karma to be the ultimate judge of a person's actions, a law has no value unless it is weighted with a recognized response (punishment). Of course breaking the law does have its own built-in punishments (karma/cause and effect) but chances are, the person who would break this law does so due to his or her ignorance of the law. Having ignorance of the law indicates an ignorance of the weight behind that law. Hence, we supplement the natural law with the clear weight of response for those who have not accepted the law and thus cannot see its built-in punishments. Our law says one should not strike one's mate. Supplementing this, the man-made law states that the abuser be imprisoned.

Consider one of the usually unspoken rules within most marriages: Neither member will strike the other. If one member beats the other, the law is broken. If that law is weighted with the response that the victim leaves, then the victim is no longer beaten. If the law is not weighted with that response, then the victim stays and is again beaten.

Now, compare the example of marriage with the ancient fertility religions. The simplest weight of law (punishment) is that of exclusion. When an abusive member of a marriage is left, the punishment is excluding the lawbreaker from the union of law (love). In the case of the ancient fertility religions, the punishment for abuse of law was often exclusion (banishment). Thus was the punishment given to for killing Juliet's cousin. Of that punishment, Romeo would have preferred death.

"Hadst thou no poison mixed, no sharp-ground knife,
No sudden mean of death, thou ne'er so mean,
But 'banished' to kill me? 'Banished'?"
—William Shakespeare, *Romeo and Juliet* 3.3

Banishment might sound like a harsh punishment. It was banishment from the love of her peers that caused Tempest to take her life, but when used against one who does not know the law, it serves only to protect. If Tempest had banished her loveless peers from her heart, they would not have been able to harm her with their words.

It is now common to hear that social clubs, popularity contests, and clicks are a bad thing in Wicca. But if you believe that, then ask yourself what value does a friendship have when you do not like the friend? What value does a religious organization have if you can not tolerate its members? What value does a religion have when its members do not share its law? Sure, this view is challenged. In *To Ride a Silver Broomstick* (Llewellyn Worldwide, 1993), Silver Ravenwolf tells us: "In the Craft, there is room for everyone."

In theory, this may be so, but all but a fool can see how inclusion lends itself to dilution. Is there room in our fertility religion for everyone? How about child molesters?

> "Never a season with a fool shall ye spend, lest be counted as his friend."
>
> —From the Wiccan Rede

That which is in and of itself love (the Law) must be willing to banish as well as welcome, divide as well as unite, such that those who seek to welcome are not banished, those who seek to unite are not divided, and those who count love as their greatest strength do not find that it is their greatest weakness.

The Sterilization of Our Fertility Religion, and the Witch War of 1971

2

All three of us continue to call ourselves Wiccan, but we do not label ourselves ANY specific tradition, regardless of our Alexandrian/Seax Wiccan roots.

—Janet Farrar, Steward Farrar (1916–2000), and Gavin Bone from their Website (*www.wicca.utvinternet.com*) January, 2002

Introduction

So Why Has Wicca Failed So Many People?

We have all heard the term *Witch War*. Usually it denotes one coven or social group bickering with another. In the extreme case of immaturity, it refers to individuals and covens casting spells of harm against each other. Usually, if you look deeply enough, you will find Witch Wars are like most conflicts, rooted in someone's lust for money or authority.

The greatest of these wars began more than 30 years ago. I turned 6 in 1971, so it is not by direct account that I relay this information. Instead, it is from reading the homespun literature of the time that I recognize this war that has led to the sterilization of our fertility religion. What do I mean by homespun? Well it is not by chance that the first major Witch War started in 1971.

More than anything else, this was a war of words, and it was just about a year earlier that those words could be distributed widely at a low cost. You see, 1970 was the year that Xerox introduced its first Electrostatic Printer.

> ➤ In 1973, Xerox introduced its first color copier, and the Witch War became colorful.

> ➤ In 1974, Xerox introduced its first high-volume copier, and the Witch War went high-volume.

Today it seems like almost every Witch calls him- or herself Wiccan. Indeed, the word has come to mean much more than it did when Wicca (as a religion) was first introduced. But that was most definitely not the case prior to the Witch War of 1971. Prior to this war, the two major players were the Hereditary Witches and the Gardnerian Witches. The Gardnerian Witches were the first to use the word *Wicca* (aka *Wica*) to refer to a specific religion. Prior to their use of the word, it was an Old English term meaning *male witch*, which is exactly how it tended to be used by the Hereditary Witches. In kind, *Wicce* was the term used to note a female Witch.

Before I explain the Witch War of 1971, I have to tell you of the first time I called myself Wiccan. It was in 1983 after having joined the U.S. Army. Although I had placed the word Pagan on the form for my dog tags, the tags were issued as "No Preference." I pointed this out to my drill sergeant. He sent me to the chaplain who asked me to describe my religion. I did, and he insisted that I was Wiccan. I tried and tried to tell him that I was not Wiccan, because the word was reserved for the either a Gardnerian Witch or a male hereditary elder, but he cited a military manual. I gave up, and my dog tags were reissued with the word *Wicca* for my religious preference. As the Pagan community started to use the word much as the military did, I accepted the title even though there is still a bit of me that thinks calling oneself Wiccan without being an elder is pompous.

Marion Weinstein (one of my favorite authors) once described a similar event in one of her comedy routines. A reporter asked her what type of Witch she was. The reporter seemed to know more about the movement than Weinstein. The reporter insisted that Weinstein be either a Feminist Dianic Witch or a Wiccan Witch, because to this reporter, those were the only two flavors of Witchcraft. This greatly surprised Marion Weinstein, because she was neither flavor.

Here, in the definitions of words, is where the Witch War of 1971 started. Not so much in the question of what is right or wrong (or why), but in who gets to decide which is the real Witch. In my example, there wasn't much to argue about. I was a soldier, and soldiers do what they are told. In Marion Weinstein's example, talking sense to the reporter was probably futile because the reporter's mind was already made up. But when one Witch argued with another Witch, failing a central authority to dictate resolve, the war flourished.

"Two households both alike in dignity,
In fair Verona, where we lay our scene,
From ancient grudge break to new mutiny,
Where civil blood makes civil hands unclean.
From forth the fatal loins of these two foes."
—William Shakespeare, *Romeo and Juliet* Prolog

The seeds of most wars are sown much earlier than the beginning of the war itself. This was the case with the Witch War of 1971, which would result in just about sterilizing our fertility religion. Although there was a short time during which the war seemed focused on the issue of homosexuality within Witchcraft, the real issue was the idea that any one person could decide who or what constitutes a "true witch." After what some estimate as little more than a mail-order course, initiation, and meeting Gerald Gardner (by some accounts only once), Raymond Buckland came to the United States, reportedly bringing with him the Gardnerian Tradition. Some publications of the late 1960s and early 1970s indicate that in the eyes of many Hereditary Witches already practicing in the United States, Buckland seemingly declared himself the Pope of all Witches. You can see how this would cause a divide between the invading Gardnerian Wicca and the Hereditary Witches already in the United States who had no connections to Mr. Gardner, much less Mr. Buckland.

> "Unfortunately (for the true witch) it is easy for
> anyone to claim to be of the Craft."[1]
>> —From *Witchcraft: Ancient & Modern*
>> by Raymond Buckland (HC Publishers, 1970)

The great bulk of this argument can be found in the word *Wicca*. If Gardner had called his tradition anything else, the war might not have begun. Buckland would have brought the Gardnerian tradition and its variants to the United States and it would have just blended with the other forms of Witchcraft already being practiced. But instead, he called it Wicca and thus gave a great many other people the idea he was speaking for a group much larger than his own tradition. So who was right? Whose tradition was "Real Witchcraft"?

Would it scare you to know that all religions are made up? That's right. In all of humanity's many views, the Creator has never handed down an instruction manual. Instead, we have received a heart and soul from which many such manuals have sprung. Some believe the age of these manuals lends to their accreditation. Others claim that ancient religions can not possibly provide for the needs of a modern people. I say they are both right. The test of time is a good challenge to any philosophy, but it is next to impossible to program a computer using only the instructions in the Bhagavad Gita or other ancient text. While this analogy might seem like a mixed metaphor, I assure you my motivation in creating *www.neopagan.com* was predominently religious in nature.

"I have been told by witches in England;
'Write and tell people we are not perverts.
We are decent people, we only want to be left alone,
but there are certain secrets that you must not give away.'"
—From *Witchcraft Today*
by Gerald Gardner (Citadel, 1954)

So the war began in 1954, but only got heated up in 1971 after Xerox introduced its first Electrostatic Printer. The religion that would change my life was invented only a decade before my birth and was sterilized when I was too young to know what sterility was.

Yes, I did say invented. Although Mr. Gardner filled our culture with the belief that Wicca had been hiding from religious persecution between the beginnings of the Burning Times and England's repeal of the final Witchcraft laws in 1952, the truth has become clear to all but our most novice. Sure, even today a few continue to cling to the idea that age lends value and that cries of persecution demand attention. There are even more than a couple authors who feed such imaginations.

"Rising from the ashes of 5,000 years of oppression and banishment to the religious underground, Neo-Paganism is now emerging as a viable body of transformative spirituality."
—From *The Truth About Neo-Paganism*
by Anodea Judith (Llewellyn Worldwide, 1994)

One is forced to wonder just what Judith considers Neo-Paganism (new Paganism) and who was persecuting those

Neo-Pagans 3000 years before the birth of Christ if not other Pagans. Although this particular example of misinformation is an extreme one, it does well to illustrate how 40 years after Gardner set the tone of victimization, we continue to cling to the victim mentality. I am sure you can see how unhealthy this is in a belief system that states like attracts like and thought tends to manifest. If you believe you are a victim, you will become a victim.

When Mr. Gardner told us that it was only the English repeal of anti-Witchcraft laws in 1952 that allowed him and others to come forward, he forgot to mention that those remaining laws dealt primarily with fraud and not with religion. Other than those laws designed to protect an innocent public from fraudulent fortune-tellers, the anti-Witchcraft laws had been abolished since 1736. I don't know about you, but I can practice Wicca just fine in a country where Ms. Cleo has to state "for entertainment only" during her TV psychic commercials. Of course, under these laws designed to protect the public, Ms. Cleo probably claims religious persecution much as Gerald Gardner did. (Have you ever heard the story of the little boy who cried wolf?)

Gardner begins his first book by telling us that he was instructed to "write and tell people we are not perverts." It has been my observation that when someone tells me that he is not a racist, that which follows seems to discount the declaration. In Gardner's case, the insistance on not being a pervert was my first clue that he was. And for the most part, the rest of his writtings confirm that hastily made assumption. Of Wiccan morality, Gardner said:

> "[Wiccans] are inclined to the morality of the legendary Good King Pausol..."
>
> —From *The Meaning of Witchcraft*
> by Gerald Gardner (Citadel, 1959)

King Pausol is a fictional character in a book titled *Les Adventures du Roi Pausole* (*The Adventures of King Pausole*). Written by Pierre Louÿs, this book describes King Pausole as having 1000 wives and promoting total sexual freedom and liberation.

Most of what Gardner described as a single tradition of Witchcraft can be found innocently enough elsewhere. But while the idea of total sexual freedom is still fresh in our minds, we can easily question his selection and combining of certain practices.

What Gardner described as Witchcraft was a system in which the coven is ruled by a single female. Within that coven, rites include nudity, bondage, blindfolding, and whipping. And yet, as the creator of the tradition, Gardner could change the rules any time he felt fit—and often did. After describing this to a friend who worked as a professional dominatrix, she summed up Gardner's efforts as: "He is topping from the bottom."

"Topping from the bottom" is a phrase in the bondage, domination, and sadomasochism (BD/SM) community to note a submissive who commands his or her dominator. Although the Gardnerian tradition has grown well beyond Gardner's original intent, it is easy to see how in Gardner's time it could be compared to a professional dungeon.

Now, don't get me wrong. I have nothing against any safe and sane practice conducted by consenting adults that involves **only** consenting adults. Remember, although BD/SM role-playing isn't one of my kinks, I'm the one with a close friend who worked as a professional dominatrix. I am no prude. However, if you are going to base your religion on it, better it be your own perversions than someone else's.

As I am sure you can imagine, many of Gardner's ideas didn't sit well with the public. As a result, his tradition did little more than occupy the time of the upper middle class English and the sensational press. This is where we can see a clear split in the paths Wicca would take. An Englishman by the name of

Raymond Buckland and a reporter named Steward Farrar would go on to create what can now be seen as the two houses of Wicca.

Buckland moved to the United States where we now know him as the author of what many of us refer to as *The Big Blue Book*, more formally known as *Buckland's Complete Book of Witchcraft*. Although Buckland had been initiated into the Gardnerian tradition, he quickly chose to part with many of the trappings of that tradition and form his own: Seax Wica (sometimes spelled Seax Wicca).

Steward Farrar remained in Europe. While working as a reporter for a newspaper called *The Reveille*, he met a hereditary witch named Alex Sanders (the founder of Alexandrian Wicca) in 1970. Mr. Sanders was so impressed by the article that Steward wrote that he invited Steward to write an informative book, which we now know and love as *What Witches Do*. Steward Farrar would not publish again until 1981.

The War Begins in the United States

The first and most powerful example of the war's U.S. origins can be found in a 1971 review of Raymond Buckland's book *Witchcraft: Ancient and Modern*:

> "First half historical rehash. Second half Buckland's Gardnerian proselytizing.
>
> "Chapter 12 'Let's All Cast Spells' takes swipes at anyone who's made a name in the Craft, to wit, any and all competitors."
>
> —From *The Wica Newsletter*, No. 5
> by Dr. Leo Louis Martello, 1971

Part of Martello's issue with Buckland's book was what Buckland considered the role of homosexuals in Witchcraft. Actually, it was more what Buckland did not consider their role:

"A 'gay witch' would be an absolute contradiction in terms. Being a religion of nature the witch is very much heterosexual; there must be a male and a female, equal numbers of each, in a coven."

—From *Witchcraft: Ancient and Modern*
by Raymond Buckland

Maybe Mr. Buckland hadn't spent enough time in nature to realize that it is filled with homosexuality. Maybe he hadn't spent enough time reading Pagan lore to realize it, too, is filled with homosexuality. As I am sure you can imagine, this statement by Buckland was widely challenged. Personally, I am still trying to figure out the whole "equal numbers" thing. At the time Mr. Buckland wrote the book, covens were typically thought to contain an odd number of members: 13. Maybe Buckland meant that someone in every coven had to be a hermaphrodite.

Back and forth it went until there was what can best be described as the start of *The War of Witches*, which not coincidentally was the headline of the newsletter in which the review of Buckland's book can be found.

Seemingly in response to *Buckland's Witchcraft: Ancient and Modern*, we see the 1971 publication of Sybil Leek's book, *The Complete Art of Witchcraft*. I say this seemed like a response to Buckland's 1970 book because Leek dedicated an entire chapter to explaining not only how homosexuality is welcome in Witchcraft, but its historical accounts.

The battle heated up at the publication of Buckland's next book, *Witchcraft from the Inside*. Here Buckland devotes just about all of Chapter 9 to again tell us who is a true Witch and who is not. While I might be inclined to respect the man for speaking his mind, he gives me the impression that he has no honor. In all his many rantings that I have read, I have not yet once seen him identify his subject by name. I do, however, get the idea that one of his targets was Sybil Leek. Of course there can be no doubt about the target when Buckland fired a shot back to England in the direction of Steward Farrar:

> "In England the main status-seeker in the pseudo-'witch' world is a man.
> He appeared claiming to be 'King of England's 30,000 witches.'"
>
> —From *Witchcraft from the Inside* by Raymond Buckland (Llewellyn Publications, 1971)

To be fair to Mr. Buckland, he does add a chapter note to the above quote that tells us that his quote was from *the New York Post*, January 28, 1966. Fortunately, I don't need the *New York Post* to know who most Wiccans would think he was talking about. That particular attack was on a Hereditary Witch named Alex Sanders (sometimes called the King of Witches). Remember that Alex Sanders initiated Steward Farrar.

By 1973, we see the war expand to include many other authors and well-known Witches. The bold headline of *Wica Newsletter* No. 22 (1973) read: "*The Witches Bible* is Bullshit." *The Witches Bible*, which was reviewed in that newsletter, was written by Gavin and Yvonne Frost and subtitled "How to Practice the Oldest Religion." On the subject of homosexuality, the Frosts' book agreed with Mr. Buckland in saying that "the practice of lesbianism and homosexuality is not condoned by Wicca." We see another connection between the Frosts and Buckland in that, like Buckland, they seemed to be speaking for all of Wicca and not just their own view on the matter. But even if they had instead said, "The Frosts do not condone homosexuality" rather than that Wicca does not, the war probably would have been furthered by their book, because many felt insulted that any Wiccan would write such drivel.

Before I list the other ideas included in the Frosts' *Witches Bible*, let me first be perfectly clear about two things: I am most certainly not talking about *A Witches Bible Complete* by Janet and Stewart Farrar. These are two entirely separate books. Second, although the Frosts made absolutely no attempt to state so, they **do not** in any way speak for all Wiccans. I, for one, hope that if they speak for any number, it be the smallest possible number.

Included in the Frosts' book are the following suggestions:

1. The hymen of female initiates be surgically broken at the earliest possible age.

2. The underside of a male initiate's penis be cut by their mothers.

3. Young female initiates be given an assortment of dildos (artificial phallus) to use in conjunction with the chart and instructions included in the book.

4. Blacks and whites shouldn't be in the same coven, partly because "Negroes have rhythm."

It is time we finally put the war to rest by recognizing what it has done.

Back in Europe With Bill the Cat

For the most part, Steward Farrar was not involved in the Witch War. This is probably both because the war was fought mainly in the United States, and because Steward was not yet in the public eye nearly as much as other authors. He had written *What Witches Do*, but he had done so at the request of Alex Sanders as an informative book about Wicca, not as an authority on the matter.

He and his wife, Janet, were handfasted in 1972, legally wed in 1975, and then moved to Ireland in 1976. Although initiated by Alex Sanders himself, after conducting research for *Eight Sabbats for Witches*, they stopped calling themselves

Alexandrian. This is a very important point. Not only did they stop calling themselves Alexandrian, they did not attempt to create another title to describe their path. Instead, they just called themselves Wiccan at a time when the word no longer denoted a specific tradition or authority. An example of their attitude can be found in the fact that they combined *Eight Sabbats for Witches* with *The Witches Way* into one book and titled the compilation *A Witches Bible* rather than *The Witches Bible*. Thus, the great bulk of Janet and Steward's writings were created after they stopped calling themselves Alexandrian.

Enter Gavin Bone, stage left. Gavin Bone became an important part of the Farrars' life, so much so that not only did he coauthor two books with them (*The Pagan Path* in 1995 and *The Healing Craft* in 1999), but he and Janet were handfasted after Steward's death.

So what does this all have to do with the Witch Wars? Well, according to Janet and Gavin's Website, Gavin was initiated into the Seax Wicca tradition in 1986, but left that tradition "after being informed that Seax Wicca was invalid as a tradition." If you don't remember from my mention previously, Seax Wicca was started by Raymond Buckland. Ah ha!

Of traditions, Janet, Steward, and Gavin agreed:

"It is important that we point out that we are honorary members of several traditions, including Strega (traditional), Eclectic Electric Eleusian Kuven (Eeek!), The Eleusian Mysteries (ATC), and The Order of Bill the Cat."
    —From their Website (*www.wicca.utvinternet.com*)
                                    as of January, 2002

The 2 Houses of Wicca

In 1971, no one could have known how much of an influence Raymond Buckland and Steward Farrar would have on the development of our religion. Today, few realize just how different these influences have been, and just about no one has observed the strange twist in those differences. Buckland became the originating point for one trend in Wicca and Farrar became the originating point for another. The twist is that the trend started by Buckland, who was initiated into the Gardnerian tradition, would result in a Wicca that is much farther removed from the Gardnerian tradition than the trend started by Steward Farrar, who was initiated by Alex and Mazine Sanders into a tradition that was reportedly a tradition with no direct ties to Gardnerian Wicca or a shared lineage. Consider the Charge of the Goddess:

> "Let my worship be within the heart that rejoiceth:
> for behold: all acts of love and pleasure are my
> rituals."
>
> —From the Charge of the Goddess
> (author unknown)

With minor differences, the Charge of the Goddess was printed in its entirety in *The Witches Way* by Steward Farrar, as well as in Sybil Leek's *The Complete Art of Witchcraft*.

If you believe everything you read, the origins of the Charge of the Goddess will be a hard thing to discover. In *To Ride a Silver Broomstick*, Silver Ravenwolf offers her own rewritten version of the Charge and tells us it was originally written by Doreen Valiente for the Gardnerian tradition. The problem with Ravenwolf's statement is that one of the few things Doreen Valiente said of the Charge of the Goddess was that she did *not* write it. Per Doreen Valiente, she *rewrote* it. Valiente also tells us that the original Charge of the Goddess was written by Aleister Crowley, then rewritten by Valiente with large inclusions from an earlier book, *Aradia: Gospel of Witches* (1899) by Charles Leland.

Of the version that appears in *To Ride a Silver Broomstick*, Silver Ravenwolf wrote:

"This variation contains the major precepts of her [Valiente's] idea, but puts it in story form. It is a beautiful tale to share with both adults and children...."

I list Silver Ravenwolf in this analogy because her version of the Charge of the Goddess best illustrates how the two houses of Wicca have divided. Her version of the Charge is completely missing the Goddess telling us that "all acts of love and pleasure are my rituals." So we can safely assume that Ravenwolf does not feel this is one of the "major precepts" of Valiente's idea. For the most part, this seems to be the case with the house of Wicca that developed following Mr. Buckland's introduction of the Gardnerian tradition to the United States.

Sybil Leek did not claim to have either written or rewritten the Charge. She simply presented it to the public in her book *The Complete Art of Witchcraft*. In that same year, Raymond Buckland's book *Witchcraft from the Inside* states of ritual nudity:

"No, the reasons for nudity are several, but sex does not enter into it."[2]

He goes on to list reasons, one being:

"The Ceremony of Drawing Down the Moon contains some words said by the High Priestess as the Goddess."

Mr. Buckland then quotes the Charge of the Goddess:

"...and as a sign that ye be free ye shall be naked in your rites..."

Well now, that's fine and dandy, but just what did all those dots in the front and back of his quote mean? To find out, we can look at the Charge of the Goddess as it was published more or less in the same year by Sybil Leek. When we look for what those dots could mean, we discover something very interesting.

Reading what Mr. Buckland said alongside the Charge as presented to us by Sybil Leek might lead one to think that Mr. Buckland was quoting out of context. Per Sybil Leek, that line appears in the context of the paragraph as:

"And ye shall be free from slavery. And as a sign that ye be really free, ye shall be naked in your rites. And ye shall dance; sing; feast; make music, and love, all in my praise."

Per Valiente, her version was practically identical to the Farrars' version, which reads:

"And ye shall be free from slavery; and as a sign that ye be really free, ye shall be naked in your rites; and ye shall dance, sing, feast, make music and love, all in my praise."

You'll note that the Valiente version presented by the Farrars is virtually identical to the Leek version. The only real changes are punctuation. In fact, if Mr. Buckland was referring Valiente's version for the Gardnerian tradition, then not only did he take a sentence out, he took only *part* of a sentence to prove a point that many would read as completely counterpointed by the rest of that very sentence.

Still, some might argue that he did not know what he was doing when he made the statement. That perhaps he was unaware of the Charge as it existed in the Gardnerian tradition. To those, I give you the oldest source on which the Charge of the Goddess was based in the rewrite by Doreen Valiente.

"And as the sign that ye are truly free,
Ye shall be naked in your rites, both men
And women also: this shall last until
The last of your oppressors shall be dead;
And ye shall make the game of Benevento,

Extinguishing the lights, and after that
Shall hold your supper thus:"

—From *Aradia: Gospel of Witches*
by Charles G. Leland

Understanding the relevance of this quote requires the understanding of the term "game of Benevento." *Aradia* was originally written in Italian. In its translation into English, the word *Benevento* could have been translated into "well wind." However, although that is the literal translation, the reference is not to the words *bene* (well or good) and *vento* (wind) individually, but to the whole word Benevento, which is the name of a town in Campania, Italy. Lore has it that in the ancient world, *Benevento* was the host to orgies, which certainly included dance, singing, feasting, making music and love. Ah, this might explain why Valiente rewrote it as she did.

What makes this source tremendously important to this debate is that although it was originally published in the late 1800s, my quote from *Aradia* is from a version released by the Buckland Museum in 1968 with new material by Raymond Buckland. So, in 1971 Mr. Buckland quoted the Charge and tells us that "sex doesn't enter into it," but in 1968, he published the origins of the Charge with reference to orgies.

On the subject of the Charge of the Goddess, two distinctly different groups of authors have also emerged. On one hand, we have Sybil Leek, Valiente, and the Farrars, who have in one form or another included a reference to sex in the Charge of the Goddess. On the other, we have Raymond Buckland, Silver Ravenwolf, and others in this trend excluding the reference to sex. Another observation to all of this is that in the Sybil Leek, Valiente, and Farrar school of thought, we see the Charge connected to the rite of initiation; in the Raymond Buckland school of thought, we see the Charge connected to the rite of Drawing Down of the Moon.

To make matters even more maddening, on the subject of when the Charge is read, Gerald Gardner's book *Witchcraft Today* is rather clear:

"Before an initiation a charge is read beginning."
—From *Witchcraft Today* by Gerald Gardner
(Citadel, 1954)

He then goes on to present only part of the Charge because he is "forbidden to give any more."

Those same two houses of Witchcraft (Buckland and Farrar) can be seen to have dissimilar trends.

House One (Farrar) and its trends:

1. The Charge of the Goddess maintains its reference to sexuality.
2. The Charge is read at Initiations.
3. Hereditary based.
4. Homosexuality is openly welcome.

House Two (Buckland) and its trends:

1. The Charge of the Goddess is stripped of reference to sexuality.
2. The Charge is read at Drawing Down of the Moon.
3. Not Hereditary based.
4. Homosexuality is either not discussed or discounted.

It is important to note that these are only trends. Most notable is the issue of homosexuality. Many authors in the second trend have never said a thing that could be considered anti-homosexual. However, most of them have never published a thing that could be considered accepting of homosexuality. Sometimes it's not in what one does say as much as in something one does not say that I take issue with.

Sterility as the Tragedy of War

It has been said that innocence is the first casualty of war. This is the case in both a war of bullets as well as a war of words. Somewhere along all the sex charts, dildos, child molestation, and homophobia brought out during the Witch War of 1971, our fertility religion was sterilized. U.S. publishers and authors probably felt it was easier to ignore those issues by removing sex from Wicca rather than address its abuse. As a result, Wicca as a sexless religion was instilled in the great majority of Wiccans long before the Farrars books became available.

Instead of spending that decade of the Witch Wars in bitter battle over which tradition was the Real Witchcraft, the Farrars dispensed with the formalities of their Alexandrian initiation and instead took it upon themselves to build on the matters of the heart. Essentially, they threw the title Alexandrian to the wind so they could build a Wicca on their own hearts rather than rigid teachings. In the end, those practices are strikingly similar to those spelled out by Gerald Gardner. So much so is this the case that I have met many people who claim to be Gardnerian, who also recommend the Farrars' books as good examples of the Gardnerian tradition. It does seem that the Alexandrian tradition has much more of a link to the Gardnerian tradition than Mr. Sanders admitted, but what is important here is that the Farrars did not simply recite that tradition. They built a heart and a soul on its foundation.

So naturally when the Farrars returned to the public eye, they brought a Wicca that was still deeply sexual. After all, matters of the heart often are. That scared many U.S. Witches—and still does. Where Wicca is seen as a religion that welcomes anyone, it is only natural that one would have a knee-jerk reaction to the inclusion of sex in Wiccan rites. After all, you wouldn't want to have sex with just anyone now, would you?

As a result, the marriage of Gavin Bone (formerly Seax Wicca, which is an offshoot of Gardnerian Wicca) and Janet

Farrar (formerly Alexandrian Wicca which was created by a Hereditary Witch) went mostly unnoticed. This is sad, because in their union, we see the story of Romeo and Juliet with a happy ending.

Gavin came from one house of Wicca and Janet came from the other house of Wicca (just as Romeo and Juliet came from opposing houses). In fiction, the house of Montague and the house of Capulet did finally unite as a result of the union between Romeo and Juliet. But it is my hope that in our real world, that union (such as the union of Janet and Gavin) is found in marriage rather than in death. For it is in the union of these two houses of Wicca that we find the survival of our religion.

Coven vs. Couple: Public and Semi-public Organizations

3

That's one thing that makes me wonder whether the old coven structure hasn't had its day. It served the purpose for which it was organized in the days when we were forced to be an underground group. I can well imagine that the coven structure was really what kept the Old Religion alive. But I think that's all changing.

—Doreen Valiente (1922–1999) speaking of covens and politics. From *Fireheart Magazine*, No. 6, interviewed by Michael Thorn in 1991

Introduction

While a member of Ar nDraiocht Fein (ADF), I invited a young lady to attend a function hosted by a local grove of ADF. "Oh, I can't," she replied, explaining that she was "a member of the Pagan Community Council of Ohio" (PCCO). I was caught completely off guard by her decline. Both ADF and PCCO are public organizations, not warring clans. In fact, Isaac Bonewits (then the Arch Druid of ADF) had been a guest at PCCO functions. I responded, "So what? I'm going and I'm a member of the National Rifle Association." She looked at me blankly, I looked at her blankly, and neither of us had a clue what the other was trying to express. Hours later, I remembered something I had read many years earlier. The young lady was confusing covens with public organizations. Covens, by their very nature, are both private and exclusive.

She declined because she felt she was a member of an organization that would frown on her participation in other organizations. I am surprised to find so many people confusing public organizations with private groups, but I realized the confusion; I could understand her concept of exclusivity. After all, when it comes to covens, it is commonly understood that these groups are exclusive not only in membership but even in physical territory, that buffer space being called "covendoms." I recall reading somewhere the claim that the house in which covens met were once no less than six miles apart, and thus the covendom extended half the distance between either.

It is very strange that so many members of our nature-based religion would buy into this very unnatural structure. Sure, we are a territorial creature. If you need proof, just try entering my home at 3 a.m. without an invitation. But we are also a communal creature. If you need proof, just dial 911 during an emergency and see how many people come to your assistance. Public organizations are the ones at the other end of that 911 call for help.

We are a circle within a circle. We are a community within a community. I am a member of humanity, of the United States, of the State of Ohio, of the City of Columbus, of my family and friends, of my marriage (should I be married), and of myself. I am a circle within a circle, and so are you.

We can unite the two houses of Wicca by recognizing what they are: two faces of the same religion. One is for the structure of public organizations; the other is for the structure of private groups (couples and families). In between, we have what I call "training covens," which assist in the transition between public and private.

Public Organizations

Where Private Organizations Begin

In my first book, *Wicca for Men*, I described covens in Creation's Covenant, my tradition (for lack of a better word) as "households," and said that they are formed out of marriage, birth, adoption, and friendship. To my surprise, I now receive countless letters that ask how to join a household in Creation's Covenant. At my store in Columbus, Ohio, one of the most popular questions asked is how to join a coven. My answer: by marriage, birth, adoption, and friendship. I further explain that covens, by their very nature, are private groups, and instead I offer contact information for public organizations. Because we live in a fast food world, very few people are happy with my answer and my encouragement to participate in public organizations to find personal unions. They want what they think is the *real thing* (covens), and they want it now. While it might be nice if such intimate connections could be ordered in a drive through window, when we consider the intricacy of the human psyche we see how one person's needs just won't make the next person very happy.

This is where public organizations come in. Although they don't offer instant kinship, they are easy to find and usually offer a common ground on which like minds can be found. I am sure you can see how one is more likely to find marriage, birth, adoption, and friendship among like minds.

As an example, let me tell you about one of these public organizations in Ohio. When I first started writing this book, the PCCO was led by a woman whose spirit was filled with fire: Leslie Payne Dauterman. Leslie left this world on July 1, 2000, but not before she illustrated a very important point. Where most Pagan organizations are overwhelmingly occupied with doing "Pagan things," Leslie reminded us that the simple act of being social is in and of itself a "Pagan thing." She organized a Pagan event that had no casting of a circle, no burning of incense, no beating of the drum, or anything that one would normally expect to find tossed into the potpourri of that which is Pagan. It wasn't an attempt to show the world how good Pagans are; it didn't involve activism, cleaning up a local park, or even improving relations with the greater community.

In fact, this Pagan event had absolutely nothing to do with anything commonly thought of as Pagan, which is why it stands out so well. Instead, she brought people together simply to be social. I do not believe a public organization could have a higher aspiration. Officially, I think it was called the Pagan Community Council of Ohio's Ice Cream Social. In her memory, I call it the Leslie Dauterman Memorial Ice Cream Social.

Of course, public organizations have other aspirations, but none higher. After all, a single person might be able to accomplish a respectable amount of public service or education but not nearly as much as several hundred—or even a handful of individuals—could. Thus, the model for a public organization is found in two symbiotic paths: It is an organization in service to its members, and it is members in service to the organization.

Listing every public organization is far beyond the scope of this book. Their addresses change from time to time, and unfortunately, some do tend to wink in and out of existence. Fortunately, there is a fantastic reference to these groups: Circle Guide to Pagan Groups. It's available from:

Circle Sanctuary
PO Box 219
Mt. Horeb, WI 53572
USA
Website: *http://circlesanctuary.org*

Circle Sanctuary is itself a public organization. However, because I have not had personal experience with the organization, I have chosen two that I know more of to illustrate the great variety of public organizations available to the seeker. These two groups are: the Church of All Worlds, and A Druid Fellowship. Both are fine organizations, but extremely different in their approach to providing public fellowship.

Church of All Worlds (CAW)

Church of All Worlds
960 Berry St.
Toledo, OH 43605-3044
USA
Website: *www.caw.org*

The members of this group are some of the finest human beings one can be fortunate to meet. Although it is a public organization as a whole, its smallest structure is a group called the *nest*, which is often private. Groups of nests join with unaffiliated members to form the CAW public face, called a *branch*. CAW does not dictate that nests be either private (covens) or public (groves), but it has been my experience that most worth their salt are private. In fact, many nests are themselves marriages and families.

This is where the rumors of CAW-sponsored orgies originated, born more in the Witch War of 1971 than in fact. You see, although it is not strictly a Wiccan organization, of all the public Pagan organizations, this is the best representation of what common sense tells us the ancient fertility religions must have been: families (nests) that gather together with other families and individuals (branches) to form a community (CAW).

A Druid Fellowship (Ar nDraiocht Fein)

ADF
c/o Raven's Cry Grove
859 N. Hollywood Way
Box 368
Burbank, CA 91505
USA

In sharp contrast to the Church of All Worlds, I list ADF. Here, too, are wonderful people, but the ADF is strictly a public organization. Its smallest structure is called a *grove*. These are groups both small and large, which gather regularly and celebrate at least the eight Sabbats publicly or semi-publicly. While deep friendships and matters of the heart most certainly form within those groves, the grove itself remains open to the public. It has been my experience that the difference between a public and semi-public ADF function is the level and nature of advertising. Generally speaking, a semi-public rite is one that has not been advertised outside of a grove. However, I have never been turned away from any grove function simply for not being a member of that grove.

This is the very nature of the ADF, as it was explained to me by its highly educated and respected founder, Isaac Bonewits. The basics of ADF rituals are such that once one is familiar with the formula, one can understand the rites as they are conducted by any ADF grove and thus feel comfortable attending any rite held by any ADF grove.

Semi-public Organizations (Training Covens)

Before I address the issue of private groups (covens vs. couples), I should address the training coven. This is a semi-public organization that might better be called a Wiccan seminary. These groups are almost a cross between a coven (family structure) and the public organization. In the next section, I will speak about covens as groups of people who come together to practice our religion with the focus of celebration rather than education. But here I address the type of group that comes together more for education than celebration.

I do not think celebration and education are mutually exclusive, but it is necessary to distinguish the difference for the purpose of discussion. A good way to understand the difference is to think of parenting and family relations. On one hand, we have the actual act of building family, and on the other hand, we have classes that teach parenting and family relations. In each, there is education on the subject of parenting, but in only one is there a safety net: If you drop a doll on its head, it does not grow up funny, and classroom marriages do not result in the real-world possibility of poor matches.

In the case of building family, some people do not attend classes or possess any formal education, yet manage well. Most often this is because they had one of the best teachers in the world: a successful parent (usually, their own). Their tradition of building family was handed down from parent to child, and chances are, grandma and grandpa were available for consultation. This is how the ancient fertility religions must have been, traditions handed down from parent to child, with little formal education in the religion.

So what happens when one does not have educators who personally have been successful in the subjects that they teach? In both situations, building family or coven, the result is most often disaster.

In the case of parenting without either formal education or good examples, good times are often few. Abused children tend to grow up to be child abusers; molested children tend to grow up to be child molesters; children of alcoholics and drug abusers tend to grow up to be alcoholics and drug abusers themselves. Social workers call this the "cycle of abuse."

In the case of covening without formal education or good examples, good times are also often few. Members of a failed coven often go on to create failed covens, and the members of those failed covens go on to create more covens destined for failure. If not for these organizations' tendency to wink out of existence rapidly, the number of covens destined for failure would increase exponentially. Even with that tendency, these so-called covens are much more abundant than functional groups. While this might not seem nearly as big a threat as having poor parents as teachers on parenthood, consider the number of books that assure potential Wiccans of the support structure offered in our community. What happens when they discover that such a support structure simply is not available?

The Wiccan community does have second and third generation members, but they are the exception rather than the rule. As a result, most so-called covens are slapped together as poorly as, well, as most marriages. This is why covens fail as often as marriages. Today, it is common to find Wiccans who have been in three or four failed marriages, just as it is common to find Wiccans who have been in three or four failed covens. I am sure you can see the irony in this. After all, these are the very real problems religions are designed to address.

This is where training covens come in: addressing the issue of not only teaching our religion, but how it can be used to establish deep interpersonal relationships. They are just as useful as those parenting classes I mentioned earlier. They are indispensable for those who have not had good examples in their lives. And while they are not absolutely necessary, they are still useful even to those who had good examples to follow.

Ah, but who should head a training coven? Well, someone with real world training, which is where the issue of coven vs. couple comes in.

Coven vs. Couple

When Gardner first introduced Wicca to the public, it was a coven-based religion. It was then said that "it took a Wiccan to make a Wiccan." Without a coven, you simply could not become Wiccan because there was no one to initiate (make) you. At the time, finding covens was difficult because they were small and secretive. In his book, *Buckland's Complete Book of Witchcraft*, Buckland describes the coven as a "close-knit group" and further explains:

"In fact, the members of your coven frequently become closer to you than the members of your own family, hence the Craft is often referred to as a 'family religion.'"

—From *Buckland's Complete Book of Witchcraft*
(Llewellyn Worldwide, 1986)

When Mr. Buckland wrote this, I doubt he could envision a day when covens were as prolific as they are today. Neither could he have known that covens would one day wink in and out of existence so fast that practically any guide to finding them would be outdated before it was printed. Today, coven calls are found in the windows of local stores, on electronic bulletin boards, and even in the forsaken spam (unsolicited e-mail that's sent to tens of thousands of people). There are exceptions, but for the most part, the coven is no longer what Mr. Buckland described.

The Gardnerian idea that Wiccans could only be found in covens was challenged by a man named Scott Cunningham. In his book *Wicca: A Guide for the Solitary Practitioner*, Cunningham focused more on heart than on formality, telling us that it took only your own heart to make one Wiccan. Cunningham presented a self-dedication ritual as well as instructions for practicing Wicca without a coven. This made our religion a viable option to even those who could not find other Wiccans.

When Mr. Cunningham wrote this book, I doubt he could envision a day when finding other Wiccans was as easy as visiting your local Pagan shop or clicking away on the Internet. Today, one need only buy a copy of *Circle's Guide to Pagan Groups* to find public organizations and Pagan contacts in the United States, Canada, and abroad.

In a time when the truth about Wicca was hardly published, Mr. Buckland presented a system in which the elders of our religion could instruct those new to the movement. In a time when books were plentiful but Wiccan contacts were few, Mr. Cunningham presented a system in which one could practice our religion without the benefit of coven, in which one depended instead on books and one's own heart for guidance. Both of those times have passed.

In Chapter 1, I pointed out that the argument about Wicca's roots will probably go on forever. When it comes to covens though, we find something really interesting. No matter which side of the argument you are on, there simply are no historical connections for covens, unless we are stuck in the Dark Ages.

Looking to Ancient Times

If our religion is ancient, then we should be able to look to the ancients to find a precedent for covens. However, there is virtually no reference to the existence of covens prior to the oppression of those ancient fertility religions. Instead, all evidence seems to indicate that pre-Christian Pagans practiced religion much in the way most religions are practiced today, with family, friends, and neighbors.

Looking to Modern Times

If our religion is modern, then it has no reason to form small, secretive groups, because we have nothing at all to hide. Covens, by the very nature of the modern use of the word, are set apart from the family. This flies right in the face of everything we claim we are attempting to re-establish.

Looking to Reality

If our religion is stuck in the Burning Times, then we are allowing it to be dictated by the very forces that we claim raped our traditions. Consider the victim of an actual rape. Yes, a criminal forced the victim to be victimized during the rape. But if the victim lives forevermore in fear, then isn't the victim allowing the rapist to continue the victimization? Yes. It takes strength to overcome and regain confidence. But knowing several people who have themselves overcome victimization, I have to conclude that those who continue to allow themselves and their religion to be victimized by something that happened several hundred years ago is an insult to the many who have overcome *real* adversity.

There are clear exceptions, but per modern use of the word, a coven is a small, secretive group that is set apart from the member's family and friends. Sure, some Wiccans do practice with their kith and kin, but for the most part, Wiccan literature is rather clear that these bonds of love are not why the coven is formed. Consider the first portion of the definition for coven found in Raven Grimassi's *Encyclopedia of Wicca & Witchcraft* (Llewellyn Worldwide, 2000):

> "COVEN is a group of people, traditionally thirteen in number, who join together to practice Wicca/ Witchcraft"

Now sprinkle in a little Raymond Buckland:

> "In fact, the members of your coven frequently become closer to you than the members of your own family…"
> —From Buckland's *Complete Book of Witchcraft*

Add a dash of Silver Ravenwolf:

> "In the Craft, there is room for everyone."
> —From *To Ride a Silver Broomstick*

Now ask yourself, if you took the sum of "everyone" and from those numbers you formed a small "group of people" who "join together to practice Wicca," is it likely that this "coven" of people would "become closer to you than the members of your own family"? Of course not. And yet, from the books that we have to read and the coven calls posted on public bulletin boards, that is exactly what it seems.

Of course, this situation does not apply only to Wiccans. There is a part of the Catholic Mass called the peace offering, in which everyone in attendance is asked to turn and offer a handshake to the people around them. Everyone shakes their neighbor's hand saying, "Peace be with you." When receiving this blessing, the scripted reply is "And also with you." The gesture is beautiful. But it is just about meaningless if those same people return home and are not willing to mow their neighbor's lawn after the neighbor breaks a leg.

If you are a member of a coven—or any religious organization, for that matter—then ask yourself why it is that you are a member of that organization. If your answer is to practice the formalities of the religion (ritual, circle, service, or Mass), then you should probably resign immediately. Why? Because the formality of practicing a religion cannot be the center of a meaningful religious experience. Worse yet, that formality can blind you from seeing what is really important: the living of that religious path. In the case of the Catholic peace offering, it is more important that the neighbor's lawn be mowed than the neighbor's hand be shaken.

There is an ancient Buddhist story that concludes that if you see the Buddha by the side of the road, you should kill him, because he will only distract you from the real Buddha that is in your own heart. I doubt the author meant that you should physically kill the imposter, but to make him dead in your eyes (banishment) or to ignore him.

If you run into a coven call in any public format, ignore it, because it will only distract you from the real coven (those who are in your heart). Instead, let it be now as it was for those ancient fertility religions on which we build. Let people come together as friends, family, and lovers, and let the generations that follow have this as our legacy: a family religion that is truly of family, not empty promises of family (covens) that are actually set apart from family.

Where Do We Begin?

So, we have joined public organizations and found people who touch our hearts. We want to form our own private organization and need a good example of how to build it. In the next chapter, I will address couples as leaders. But here, let's address the couple's relationship (family) as an example of what we hope to build.

I recently attended the legal handfasting of a close friend and his partner. After the rite, I sat and chatted with the Priestess who conducted the ceremony. From conversation I learned that the Priestess was currently unwed, divorced thrice, and was battling Children and Family Services for the return of her three children after one of them was sexually abused by a former lover of the Priestess. Call me a right-winger if you will, but I just can't see how a person like this should conduct marriages in a religion that teaches like attracts like.

Two other friends recently divorced each other. Although neither is Wiccan, the events leading up to their divorce serve to illustrate an important point. When their 12-year relationship started to fail, he went to see a counselor and she sought advice from a friend. It is now a year after their bitter breakup and the displacement of their 11-year-old child, and no one has questioned the poor logic in their choices of confidants. The counselor he went to had never been married, much less raised a child. The friend she went to was divorced twice and was in the steps leading up to her third divorce.

We begin with common sense. If the living of our religion is truly more important to us than the picturesque formalities of ritual, then we should begin by finding examples for the family we hope to build in the families that have already been successful. Where do we find the best example for a private organization?

➤ **Example A: Coven Whatever**

Coven Whatever is headed by Lord and Lady Whatever. They came together for the purpose of forming a Wiccan Coven. They celebrate holidays together because that is what books about Wicca tell them they should do.

➤ **Example B: Functioning Family**

The family is headed by Functioning Father and Functioning Mother. They came together for the purpose of forming family. They celebrate holidays together because they love each other.

So, which is the better example of a Wiccan Coven/Household? Coven Whatever, which is most certainly Wiccan (they profess it at every chance), or the Functioning Family, who might not profess being Wiccan, but who certainly demonstrate the very heart of Wicca? Which is more important, that handshake in the church or helping your neighbor in time of need? Which is more important, coven or family? If you have difficulty answering this question, then ask yourself who is going to mow your lawn when your leg is broken?

Of course, we do not all come from perfect families. Indeed, many have come to Wicca because it offers an alternative to dysfunctional families. Many Wiccans have turned to our religion to break that cycle of abuse that I mentioned earlier. These are people who have been abandoned, but do not want to abandon; abused, but do not want to abuse; raped, but do not want to rape; people who have not been loved, but who desperately seek to love and to be loved. For these people, those of us who *have* good role models must *become* good role models.

And what of the people who want to abuse, abandon, and rape? What of these people who do not want to love or be loved? To those who believe these conditions cannot change, I say: Do not try to change them, because one cannot if he believes he cannot. Instead, avoid these people, for they are a plague on the healthy relations that you form. To those who believe these conditions can be changed, I say: If it is in your heart and power to save them from these states, then do so, but at your own risk. A charitable heart is a good thing, but not when that charity brings harm to others. Do not let your heart welcome a child molester into your home, if doing so places your own child at risk.

Couple Instead of Coven

Better we build our religious organizations as did the ancient fertility religion: modeled after successful couples that we know personally; and better it be households we build rather than covens. Again, here we see a circle within a circle rather than isolated and mutually exclusive groups. So much is this the case that it is really hard to decide where to begin talking about this concept. Consider the typical marriage of a single man to a single woman.

A man from Family A is married to a woman from Family B. The result is Family A exists as one circle, Family B exists as circle, the Family formed by the whole of both A and B is a circle, and the man and woman form Family C as yet another circle. Circles within circles.

One might argue that this approach limits Wiccans to only marry Wiccans. Of course it does, but I say this not because I am Wiccan, but because of what is in the heart. In Wicca, each person must decide with their own heart that which is ethical. To wed someone whose ethics are not compatible will not a compatible union make.

As example, I give you one of my personal ethics drawn from our law: I believe racism is contrary to our law, hence a marriage between me and a member of the KKK would be ill fated. Now I might someday meet a woman who professes to being Wiccan, but who is also a member of the KKK. Maybe she is a member of someone else's Wicca, but certainly not mine. Wicca is in the heart.

In kind, it does not matter what religion is practiced by the families. It is more Wiccan that I sit down to dinner with my Catholic mother for what she calls Christmas than attend ritual with Lord and Lady Whatever for what they call Yule. Further, spending holidays with Lord and Lady Whatever lends itself to alienating one from the folk who really matter, those in one's heart.

Instead, we should become involved in public and semi-public organizations for education and social functions, but form the religious organizations (covens/households) that really matter of those who are close to our hearts, and model those private groups on successful families.

If Wicca is to be anything more than the latest fad, we will continue to grow. In a couple of generations there will be many Wiccan households formed out of marriage. Some of these households will welcome birth, adoption, and friendships. Our more formal rites will then be performed by and with those we love, and Wicca can truly be more of the heart than of fashion. But this will only happen if we choose couple over coven as our religious structure.

Wiccan Leaders: Guru, Clergy, or Couple?

4

> *Once upon a time in a far away land,*
> *there lived a princess of incomparable beauty.*
> *Although she seemed to have*
> *everything a girl could want—friends,*
> *riches, servants, and so forth—she was*
> *absolutely miserable.*
>
> —From *Enchantments of the Heart,*
> by Dorothy Morrison (New Page Books, 2001)

Introduction

Aside from the heads of our public, semi-public, and private organizations, the Wiccan community has a variety of public leaders. Call them spokespeople if you like. More often than not, the better-known spokespeople are our authors. Some of these folks have risen to near fame in the Wiccan community—and that alarms me.

Wicca is a minority religion. As such, Wiccan authors do not make much of an income from writing. Instead, our motivation has to be found elsewhere, or we burn out. Part of my motivation is in the perks of being an author. One of those perks is that authors tend to be sought-after speakers. In my case, this is perfect because I love to meet new people. For every hour I spend speaking, I have many hours of listening to look forward to. This, more than any other reason, is why I continue to write, because I am given the opportunity to meet my readers and hear their thoughts, ideas, and concerns. To be honest, although the Leo in me does sometimes enjoy the spotlight, I am always absolutely terrified the moment before I open my mouth before an assembly of my peers.

It was during one of those terrified moments that I was struck with a tremendously humbling thought. I stood before a group of university students in Fort Wayne, Indiana, when it sunk in; I am a high school drop out with very little college education. In front of me was a group of people with much more education who had gone out of their way to hear me speak. More humbling was the fact that their university had paid me to be there. My heart sunk and I thought for sure I would botch the presentation.

To my great surprise, it went well. My muse spoke silently in my ear, and I repeated what she said to the group. After my words, a group of us went out for fries and shakes, and I received the real benefit, the reason I always welcome such invitations: their words. The next day, I raced home to make changes to this chapter, based on what I'd just experienced.

This is the relationship I think Pagan authors should have with their readers: one part talking and many parts listening. Much like the bards and storytellers of old who brought news and new ideas from one village to the next, we should serve to chronicle the Pagan community's growth and diversity rather than dictate it. Pagan authors should, in essence, be the storytellers and not the leaders. After all, our religion may be spread by stories and myths as it was with the religions of old, but the storyteller is not the story. In our fertility religion, the story is the couple itself.

Having spent only a few years abroad, I know very little of the Pagan movement in Europe. What I have observed leads me to believe that we have experienced much more of a revolution here in the United States than they have abroad. In Germany, it seems the movement is more of a re-emergence than a revolution. There, much of the "what" of the Pagan movement has gone on mostly unchallenged from its ancient roots, but during my few years there, it was clear that the "why" of those ancient traditions was beginning to show itself to the masses.

Perhaps this is why Wicca in the United States has all but formally adopted the words of Lady Liberty (the Statue of Liberty):

"Give me your tired, your poor. Your huddled masses yearning to breathe free..."

I am not aware of statistics to either prove or disprove what I have observed in the Wiccan community. Truth be known, there are many stable and prosperous Wiccans, and this might just be a matter of the squeaky wheel getting oiled first. But a quick glance at the people who call themselves Wiccan might lead one to believe we are not exactly the most stable people in the world. A closer examination might show that the only thing more common among Wiccans than antidepressants is perpetual poverty.

Of course it looks that way. We welcome anyone who would join our fold and then provide them with absolutely no sense of leadership, no examples by which they can improve their lives. Those who are stable and prosperous tend to remain in their world of stability and prosperity, leaving the rest of us to try and sort our way out of this mess without so much as guidance.

Yes, I did say the rest of "us," because although I might steer clear of antidepressants, I do not count myself as stable and most certainly not prosperous in most senses of the word.

"America's New Niggers..."

I recently heard a horrible joke that sums up what is happening in Wicca today.

Question: Why can Wiccans make love all night but Christians can't?

Answer: Because Christians have to go to work in the morning.

The joke itself wasn't new to me. I had heard practically the same joke many years earlier, only then it was the "white man" that couldn't make love all night because he had to go to work in the morning. Indeed, it does seem that because racism is now recognized as a no-no, another type of prejudice is showing its nasty little head:

> "America's new niggers are minority religious groups, especially the disorganized WICCA."
> —From *Wica Newsletter* No. 18, by Leo Martello
> (date uncertain, probably 1972 or 73)

I draw attention to this problem not to shame us, but because I believe that recognizing a problem is the first step in changing it. Consider all of the anti-gay and anti-lesbian feelings that were expressed within our movement back in the 1970s (see Chapter 2). Today, it has become clear that homophobia is what is not welcome. The change in thinking came about when the gay and lesbian community became "Out, Proud, and Free." By welcoming them, we gained their strength and too became Out, Proud, and Free (hence the saying "Out of the Broom Closet"). Indeed, if we look to other minority communities, we can see what has worked and what has not.

Nowhere is this practice more important to our fertility religion than in the area of the families and relationships that we build. After all, isn't that what it is all really about? Nowhere has this been more publicly discussed than in another minority community: in this case, the African-American community.

There we see a rushing forth of authors and spokespeople who insist that the great majority of current problems facing the African-American community are found in the families and relationships that African-Americans form. Although the African-American community continues to experience greater levels of poverty than the European-American community, the financial distance between the two is greatly reduced between married African-American couples and married European-American couples. This should not come as a surprise when we consider the fact that, regardless of race, most truly successful people list a loving spouse as the key to their success.

Of course some will say that we should remain isolationists. But even as isolationists, are we not ourselves gay, straight, white, black, and all things in between? Are we not still a circle within a circle? Hence, in looking to other minorities for examples of what has worked and what has not, we are looking to our own community.

As with the African-American community, we do not all have great role models for building families. So, like the African-American community, many of us turn to public figures to show us the path to success.

Who Best to Represent Us?

> "Those who do not remember their history are doomed to repeat it."
>
> —A Jewish Proverb

When we think about leaders, we tend to think in terms of people who are appointed by some force beyond our control. That idea is reinforced everywhere we look. You might own stock in one company or another, but unless you are one of the elite few, you don't have enough power to steer policy. The political arena is worse. I can think of no better example than the U.S. presidential election of 2000. Some think the presidency was stolen, others think the rightfully elected person got the job. The truth of the matter is that we all lost. We, the people, lost a bit of the sense that we could make a difference, that our vote actually counted for something.

Wicca is not corporate, and it is not politics. Oh, we do have elections for offices in public organizations, and some of those organizations have incorporated, but while those organizations might *represent* Wiccans, they are not in and of themselves Wicca.

One of the many ways Wicca differs from other religions is in our selection of public leaders. Simply put, we have no set policy for selecting leaders. As a result, we have a community with leaders who are both poorly educated (I'll call these our gurus) and well-educated (I'll call these our clergy). Unfortunately, where we sought to avoid the mistakes of other religions by not establishing clear criteria for our leaders, the result is that we are destined to repeat the mistakes of both. In effect, our inaction has become the action, consigning us to repeat the very mistakes of others that we aimed to avoid.

On Gurus

In context of its Hindu and Tibetan Buddhist origin, the word *guru* refers to a personal spiritual leader, teacher, trusted advisor, and mentor. Even outside of its original use, it sometimes has a positive meaning. On Wall Street, it would be a high compliment to call someone a "Financial Guru." But that is not case with the one I call the Wiccan Guru.

We have all met him. Oftentimes he is the one sending out those public coven calls that I mentioned earlier. Other times, he is the tormented poet-philosopher who we meet in a local coffee house or favorite bar. His story is always the same: He is a noted expert on just about everything, but all of the world stands against him because they just aren't willing to see the truth. He is the outsider, the person no one understands, and chances are he is very attractive to you because you count yourself as much an outsider as he does.

That kinship we feel when we meet this guru often masks the fact that his poetry and philosophy are simply poorly crafted. His life is either in neutral or reverse, never improving on his state of being. He desperately seeks others while professing his independence. He is the Wiccan equivalent of the sidewalk preacher, forever searching for people who will agree with his distorted and sometimes false sense of reality.

If that were where his story ended, he wouldn't pose much of a threat to the Wiccan community. He would continue to be worshipped in small circles, but eventually his credibility would be seen for what it is, and his "students" would move on. Unfortunately, his story doesn't always end there.

Just like that Financial Guru, there are organizations out there who give the Wiccan Guru a sense of heightened credibility. In the world of finance, the guru gains credibility from financial institutions. They make money from your purchases and sales when you work with their guru. In Wicca, the guru is often an author, who gains credibility when his or her ideas are published. The institution that makes money here (other than the author) is the publishing house.

The main difference between the Financial Guru and the Wiccan Guru is that, generally speaking, the Financial Guru is chosen by an institution that usually understands and works with finance, but the Wiccan Guru is chosen by an institution of which it's members are usually not Wiccan, nor have much knowledge about the religion. As a result, those who become Wiccan authors are sometimes good for the community, but sometimes they are not. I am sure you can see how this is not the best method by which to select our public leaders.

One might argue that a guru's career is only initiated by the institution, but ultimately it is what is held within the books that will bring the guru into popularity and thus, a role of leadership. But if that is the case, one must ask who it is that is purchasing the books written by these poor leaders. Truly successful books on Wicca rise in sales not from how they perform within the Wiccan community, but how they sell in mainstream book-stores (where people into Wicca as a fad tend to shop). Do we really want our public leaders to be dictated by the mainstream?

Making matters even worse, books that tell us what we want to hear are more likely to sell in any store, but is that a good role for a leader? As a child, you may have wanted to play with a hot pot on the stove but did not because your mother told you what you did not want to hear: "No." And that is exactly what we should be telling our gurus. No. We, as a community, should demand better leadership.

On Clergy

One might think the solution to the problem with gurus is to insist that our leaders be educated. But what exactly is an education, and how do we certify its authenticity? I challenge you to prove Gerald Gardner's degree, and wonder why it is that so many of our authors once published with the title "Dr." before their names, but later dropped such formalities. As a parody of this trend, I have even toyed with the idea of listing myself as A.J. Drew, Bhg. (Big hairy guy), but that might be a bit over the top.

One might argue that we need state-recognized clergy to perform legal handfasting. On this point, it is impossible to argue, but this is no more a role of leadership than the role played by a notary.

On the other hand, some think a minister's license elevates one to leader status, but that just flings the door open to abuse.

Most states have laws similar to what Gardner claimed England repealed, thus allowing his books on Witchcraft to be published. These laws attempt to prevent unaccredited people from calling themselves counselors. Usually this is accomplished by imposing a state certification or license on anyone who would use the word for business purposes. This is a good thing; it attempts to protect the general public from paying for bad advice. The exception to this law is the religious freedom given by the Constitution of the United States. Most states also allow everyone with a minister's license to call themselves counselors, charge for their services, and dispense whatever advice they choose, without much fear of a medical malpractice suit.

Many women have had the misfortune of this abuse of religious freedom when they sought counseling on the issue of abortion. Instead of receiving a fair and balanced overview of their choices, many "clinics" have set up to preach religious views under the guise of legitimate counseling. No matter how one feels on the issue, no one should be deceptive in their dispensing of advice on it.

But even with both a minister's license and a verifiable education, oftentimes counselors are lacking in practical experience. When it comes to marriage counseling, the Catholic Church couldn't be more misguided. Sure, their priests have formal education and on-the-job training, but (with few exceptions) they are unwed, celibate, and have taken an oath of poverty. Therefore, they are not qualified in real-world experience with marriage or sex. Nor are they qualified with real-world experience in what many couples argue about: money. Someone who has taken an oath of poverty is not the right one to council on that matter. Without practical experience, how can these people provide expert advice?

So Where Do We Find Leadership?

As the African-American community discovered with the murder of Martin Luther King, Jr., our earthly leaders can be taken away from us. In this type of loss, we realize that the earthly representatives are merely spokespeople for our real leaders.

Personal real leaders are not appointed by corporate officers, they are not selected by democratic vote, and they most certainly are not self-appointed. They need no license, certificate, or proof of education. They need not be sanctioned by local, state, or federal government. Instead, our leaders are defined by those who would follow them. That's right, when it comes to selecting leaders, you are in complete control. Who better to make such decisions?

So who then should be the earthly representatives of our leaders? Well, where do you want to be led? If you want to become a successful computer programmer, you should look to successful computer programmers to find your leader. If you want to be a successful football player, find a coach who was once a successful football player. A mechanic, find a mechanic. In all things, we should look for guidance in those who have demonstrated success in the field in which we seek guidance.

Couples as Wiccan Leaders

The spokespeople in any community who point out the need to address family and relationship issues are not the real leaders. Instead, the real leaders in a community are the couples who have either heard the message and took heed, or those who knew the message long before it was spoken. So, too, should it be in the Wiccan community.

The real leader is the Creator, which is in and of itself love, because no matter who tells you what you should do, ultimately it is only what is in your heart that will guide you.

Here we are again challenged to redefine Wicca. If it is a social statement, I imagine you could find your leaders in the social elites. If it is a fashion statement, you can find them in the fashionable. But if you feel as I do, that we are separated (from our Savior/other half) for the sake of union and that Wicca is the best path by which you can find that union, then look to your own heart for guidance, look for spokespeople among the people who have already found what is in your heart, and ultimately look to love for leadership.

Let me tell you of one of my personal leaders, an earthly representative of the Goddess herself: Dorothy Morrison. You might know her as the wildly successful author of the book *Everyday Magic*. But it isn't for her writing of *Everyday Magic* that I call her my personal leader. To be honest, that isn't even my favorite book by her pen. Of her many books, I much prefer *Enchantments of the Heart*. But even that book is not why I count her as one of the best examples of public leaders.

I look up to her and count her as one of the best Wiccan leaders because I knew her long before she had the motivation to write *Enchantments of the Heart*. That motivation can be found in the book's dedication to her husband, Mark, whom Dorothy says reminds her that:

> "True love and romance are not only the ultimate magics, they are alive and well and dancing in our hearts..."

Now, tempting as it might be to idolize people who are in healthy relationships, that is not why I put Dorothy on a pedestal. After all, what, of becoming rich, can one learn from someone who has always been rich? Instead, I do so because she has not always been in a healthy relationship. Like many of us, she has been beaten and put down, treated miserably, and become bitter for it. But somewhere in her heart she found the ability to love again. I look up to her and her husband, Mark, because they have overcome separation and found union of a kind I can at this time only imagine.

So let our public leaders (spokespeople) be the earthly representatives of the love between our Lord and Lady. At present, I know of only Dorothy and Mark who have been as public with their love, so for the rest of you... come out, come out wherever you are.

You see, we have all come to this religion searching for something. Like attracts like. Now that some of us have realized what it is, we need to know how to find it, and more importantly, how to keep it.

How Much Is That Goddess in the Window: Archetype or Stereotype?

5

"It is important to know the various deities as they are! I am extremely offended when someone makes up a Goddess and slaps an ancient name on Her.
For example, although she is glorious in her own right, the Morrigan is not a sweetness and light Mommy.
Yet I have seen her described that way."

—From *The Heart of Wicca*
by Ellen Cannon Reed (Weiser, 2000)

Introduction

As Dorothy and Mark's love points out, fairy tales can come true. But fairy tales do not always have happy endings. Call them what you will: fairy tales, mythology, or archetype, in addition to the real-world examples that we see all around us, we have a vast amount of information in which we can find both aspirations and warnings. But we will find neither if we choose not to look.

Ask yourself who your favorite Goddess form is. Write it down on a piece of paper along with your reasons for choosing her as a personal archetype. When you have listed at least three reasons, then do the same for your favorite God form. Compare the two names. Are they from within the same pantheon? If so, were they lovers? Are any of your reasons for choosing them because they represent the type of loving relationship that you seek? If you answered these questions as most Wiccans do, at least one of the answers was no.

Try another exercise. Make a list of all the Goddess forms that you can think of. Then make a list of all the God forms that you can think of. Compare the two lists and see if you, as most Wiccans, have remembered many more names for our Lady than for our Lord.

One last exercise. Make a list of all the Gods and Goddesses who are couples. Inevitably this list will be far shorter than either your list of Goddesses or Gods. This demonstrates where the focus of Wicca has been placed. First on Goddess, then on God, and finally on the union of God and Goddess. In all of our claims that Wicca is a fertility religion, we seem to have managed to place its focus on individuals rather than couples. Just how fertile can a solitary individual be?

Although I prefer the conversations that I find on the chat network that I am building,[1] every now and then I like to poke around the chat rooms of America Online. Sometimes I don't type much, preferring instead to read what AOL Witch A is arguing about with AOL Witch B. More often than not, what I find when I enter a Wiccan chat is not talk on the incarnations of our many deities, but rather talk of the many incarnations of Star Trek.

It was during one of those visits that I met an AOL Witch whose screen name included the word Shiva (I am withholding the exact screen name). Because I hold our Lord Shiva and his Lady Parvati in very high esteem, I asked her why it was that she included his name in hers, thinking perhaps I'd found a like soul, even if there was a matter of gender bending (Shiva being male). She hadn't a clue.

Not only did she not know of Shiva's great stories, but she insisted that he was actually female, which, knowing his reputation, might not be a good thing to do. Thinking perhaps there might be a female archetype by the same name but of a different pantheon, I inquired further and discovered she had confused Shiva (a Hindu God) with Bast (an Egyptian Cat Goddess). How you might ask? Well, my best guess is that she saw a commercial for Sheba cat food by Kal Kan Foods, Inc. The names must have sounded familiar, and there you have it. A new Goddess is born partly of the Hindu pantheon, partly of the Egyptian pantheon, but mostly of a can of cat food.

Now don't get me wrong. I see absolutely nothing wrong with inventing personal deity forms. In fact, if you looked at my altar this very moment, you would see that our Horned God now rides a Harley Davidson. This is as it was. Not only did ancient communities often have Gods and Goddesses unique to their small village, but individual craft folk had Gods and Goddesses unique to the individual. The practice of kiln gods is still in use today by many potters (this one included). However, if these created deities are the only ones of our concern, we miss out on a great deal of guidance found in the ancient stories belonging to the Gods and Goddesses as envisioned by others.

In our many rituals, our Lord and Lady are sometimes seen as the nameless ideal masculine and feminine. This is the case with the union of athame and chalice, as I have never met a Wiccan who has given deity names to his or her tools. Here we are reminded of the sanctity of life and the blessings of union. In some rites, we associate deity with the stages of life. Our Lady as Maiden,[2] Mother, and Crone, and our Lord as Master, Father, and Sage. Here we see the lesson that life is a cycle of birth, life, and death. But beyond those basic concepts, we seem not to look further.

The Generic Deity

Wiccan altars are typically decorated with generic symbols of our Lady on the left, generic symbols of our Lord on the right, and generic symbols of their union in the center. Some of these symbols move during ritual to note the transformation between separation and union. This is the case with such objects as salt and water. Water represents the womb of Goddess and salt represents the semen of God. Before union, a vessel of water is placed on the left side of the altar and salt on the right. When salt is added to water, the vessel in which it was mixed is placed in the center of the altar. This is a beautiful practice that reminds us that our rites praise the union of Lord and Lady rather than Lord or Lady alone.

Other items used to represent our Lady include (but are not limited to): chalice, pentacle, cauldron, and shed seashell, as well as stones and herbs that are associated with the female gender.

Other items used to represent our Lord include (but are not limited to): athame, censor, sword, wand, and shed antler, as well as stones and herbs that are associated with the male gender. These are normally selected in accordance with personal views. As an example, I said "shed antler" as opposed to "antler" because I am a vegetarian.

The Three Stages of Life

In many of our rites, we honor the different stages of life as represented by our Lady as Maiden, Mother, and Crone, as well as our Lord as Master, Father, and Sage. Here we tend to connect celestial symbols more so than altar tools and orna-ments. This is the case in our Lady's representation in the New, Full, and Dark moon, much as it is in the case of our Lord's representation in the New, Full, and Dark year.

Specific Deities and Their Relationships

However, if we are to look to our Lord and Lady for any guidance beyond the introduction of the basic principles of union and the cycles of life, we must look to our Gods and Goddesses on a more personal level. On that level, we can get to know them better and begin to create our personal relationship with their many forms. Here we see that our Lord and Lady are not exactly what we have seen in their generic form. On a personal level, we see that our Lady is not always associated with the Moon and our Lord is not always associated with the Sun. In fact, there are many Sun Goddesses and many Moon Gods to be found in Pagan lore.

We can also see a tremendous divergence from the idea that our Lady in her incarnation is the all-pleasant, happy, joyful mother of the universe. We see the role of mother as that of defending her children, sometimes with the use of extreme force. Here we see that our Lord is not always the completely devoted husband to our Lady, but that oftentimes his fancy does wander. On the personal level, we see that our Lord and Lady are not always the perfect archetype that we sometimes envision. And this is a good thing, because having more in common with our Gods and Goddesses allows us to become closer to them. We make mistakes just as they do. We feel the result of those mistakes just as they do. But unlike them, we have their many examples on which to draw.

Wiccans do tend to decorate their altars and homes with the images of specific Gods and Goddesses. But when we consider how we answered the questions in the introduction to this chapter, it is not surprising that these specific deities are often from dissimilar pantheons. Although there is nothing wrong in this if done for art's sake, it might indicate a trend towards objectification. Again we look to past events to assist our future endeavors.

Woden and Frig

Consider the use of Woden and Freya in Raymond Buckland's Seax Wica. Instead of the lore of Woden and his wife Frig, Mr. Buckland choose Woden and Freya because:

> "Unfortunately 'frig' has certain connotations today which would be misplaced!"
>
> —Buckland as originally quoted by
> *Earth Religion News*, (Yule 1973)

Indeed, the fourth edition of the American Heritage Dictionary does give two meanings for the word *frig*:

1. To have sexual intercourse with.

2. To perform an act of masturbation on.

To those who would argue the incorrectness of Mr. Buckland's choice, he says:

> "Any comment regarding their being 'incorrect' is, then totally erroneous."
>
> —From *Buckland's Complete Book of Witchcraft*

He must have seen me coming. What is erroneous here is the idea that we can separate our archetypal couples without removing their attributes as a couple. Again, there is nothing wrong in decorating our homes with images from different pantheons, but if we look to those images outside of the archetypes that they represent, then we are assigning our own stereotypes rather than consulting their archetypes.

In kind, if we mismatch deity forms, we remove their ability to provide the archetypal advice available from their stories. While it might seem more politically correct to use Freya and Woden, in so doing, one only receives the benefits of Woden's story and Freya's story, but not the story of the union as husband and wife—Woden and Frig.

I count myself blessed for having come from a home in which my father and mother deeply loved each other. I count myself again blessed for having a couple like Dorothy and Mark to look up to. But my parents weren't perfect in all matters; Dorothy and Mark didn't know each other a few years ago; and many of us do not have such examples in our lives. Rather than poke around in the dark, Wiccans have other sources from which to draw.

Here, again, our modern religion can look to the ancients for guidance. The myths and stories of the ancients are not just entertainment. The deities in those myths are not just pretty images for our altars or homes. They are guides and warnings that can be incorporated into our modern religion, because they are timeless. Men have always been men, women have always been women, and the basic challenges confronted by men and women have remained relatively unchanged throughout time. But when we only listen to one side of the tale (be it God or Goddess), we aren't getting the whole story, and are thus denying ourselves the guidance that their interaction offers.

Hera and Zeus

Consider Hera and Zeus. If we look at Hera outside of her relationship with Zeus, we don't see the many indiscretions of Zeus, and thus we have no explanation for Hera's actions against Titaness Leto, Callisto, Semele, Aigina, or Alkmena. But when we have Zeus in the picture, we know that these were his many mistresses that his wife so despised. Without Zeus, we have no idea why Hera also persecuted Epaphus, Arkas, Dionysus, Aiakos and (most notably) Herakles. But with Zeus in the picture, we know that he is the father of each, but not by Hera. The story of Hera and Zeus is of jealousy, and a warning of what happens when couples are mismatched in their choice of monogamy—or perhaps a story of what happens when a couple is not open and honest with each other.

Shiva and Parvati

What about Shiva and Parvati? Alone, Shiva is often seen as the destroyer, but when united with Parvati in her incarnation as Shakti, we typically see Shiva in the very act of creation (the Great Rite). When we see Kali (another incarnation of Parvati) alone, we see another destroyer. But when Shiva comes into the picture, we get a different story. You see, Parvati only became Kali as a result of trying to save lives.

The story has been repeated with many variants, but the sum is that several countrymen went to Parvati asking for protection from invading demons. The mortals couldn't kill the demons because whenever they spilled the demons' blood, more demons were born of the blood striking the earth. Defending the country folk was normally a role played by Shiva, so in his absence, Parvati told the countrymen that she would unroll her tongue on the earth. They should trick the demons onto her tongue, where the demons could be killed without fear of their blood striking the earth. She would then bring her tongue back into her mouth, destroying the demons. Everything went as expected until Parvati had a reaction to the demons' blood, which brought her to a killer's rage and transformed her into Kali. This is where Shiva comes in.

Upon his return, Shiva saw what had become of his beloved. No mortal could stop Kali's rage, so Shiva threw himself at her feet. Because Shiva is a God, Kali could not destroy him. Instead, by one account, she is forever trapped trying to destroy him—rage balanced by sacrifice. By another account, Kali became tired of trying to kill Shiva and returned to being Parvati.

So, Shiva without Shakti is often seen as the destroyer. With Shakti, he is a Creator. Shiva without Kali is also often seen as the destroyer. With Kali, he is a sacrificial god, offering his own life as the salvation of his countrymen.

Personal Relationship With Deity

Wiccans, like members of other religions, have personal relationships with the Creator in its many forms. We might be called "idol worshipers," but such statements only demonstrate ignorance. If Wicca is in the heart, then we have no great attachment to idols. Instead, we have great attachment to those whom the idols represent.

As a fertility religion, we should seek to develop personal relationships with our Gods and Goddesses because in learning about these Gods and Goddesses, we learn about the people with whom we seek earthly personal relationships. To seek to do otherwise is about the same as forming relationships based on looks alone. If that be done, the relationship is doomed to fail much the way Wicca will fail if we choose archetypes based on similar superficial attributes.

What Is Totally Erroneous.

What is totally erroneous. Note the period at the end there. It is not a question. It is a statement. The what of our deities is not important. Instead, it is the why that is important. When we look at the why, we find that Mr. Buckland selected Woden and Freya because he was worried someone might be offended by the name Frig, rather than using Frig because she and Woden have a story to tell.

6

The Magickal Child: Wiccan Rituals vs. Real Life

A magickal pattern or relationship is
what happens when you take
love and sex and tap into its source, giving the
experience divine and spiritual properties.

—From *Love, Sex, and Magick*
by Sirona Knight (Citadel Press, 1999)

Introduction

Before we get started, I have to tell you of a term I am going to introduce in this chapter: *initiated to*. It notes that the united couple is sexually active, and it means much the same as the biblical reference "to know." In using this term, I am most certainly not trying to imply that in order to be Wiccan one must first be initiated by sex. Instead, this is a comment on the relationship between Host (priest) and Hostess (priestess). It is the difference between the sex routinely shared by a loving couple (initiated to each other), and the first time they shared each other's bodies in such a way as to initiate the bonds that are known only by lovers.

In Chapter 2, I told you about two books with similar names. They are: *The Witches Bible* by the Gavin and Yvonne Frost, and *A Witches Bible Complete* by Janet and Steward Farrar. One of the reasons I stated for not being all that fond of the Frosts' book was that their title started with "The," and thus indicated that it spoke for all Wiccans. On the other hand, the Farrars' book title starts with the word "A," to indicate that they do not speak for all Wiccans. One might then think that Wiccans do not have a common bible. In truth, we share no sacred text as a bible. However, we do indeed share what might be called a common bible.

Our bible is easy to miss because it isn't found in every hotel room. But it is there nonetheless. You see, our bible isn't so much a collection of words on paper as it is a collection of stories told in our rites. Our bible is the sum of our rituals (sacred theater). While these rituals may change from one Wiccan to the next, their similarities are at least as many as those found between one version of the Christian Bible and another. Much the way other religions tell their stories in holy scripture, our religion tells its story in sacred theater (rituals). Where different denominations of other religions choose different versions of their bible, we choose different versions of ritual between different Wiccan groups.

Of course, this means that just as other religions have fanatics who insist their particular choice of scripture and their interpretation of that scripture is fundamentally true, we have fundamentalists who believe their particular choice of ritual and their interpretation of those rituals are just as fundamentally true. This is a very dangerous path on which to tread, because those who would follow such a path are certainly doing so because their minds simply cannot accept paradox. Thus, they are ill-prepared when two seemingly different truths are uncovered.

Consider the Great Rite, or symbolic Great Rite, which is central to all Wiccan rituals. Because it represents the union between man and woman, a fundamentalist Wiccan might take the stance that homosexuals and lesbians are not welcome in Wicca. But what, then, of the Charge of the Goddess that tells us that "all acts of love and pleasure" are the Goddess' rituals?

Well, one can just choose to ignore the inference entirely, or pick and choose what he or she likes, casting the rest aside and hoping no one notices (we noticed). Or one can do as the Farrars choose and say: "This is how I see it," rather than to say, "This is how it is," and let the paradox be addressed by those whom it pertains to. With that said, this chapter will present my take on the basic structure of Wiccan ritual and its relation to real life. This is how I see it.

The Magickal Child

Which is more important, ritual or life? When we see rituals for what they are, we understand how their meaning is absolutely lost without the context of the importance of life. Rituals are a celebration of that life, where athame joins chalice. The union of man and woman (Lord and Lady), as well as the fruit of that union, is celebrated. That fruit is the *magickal child*.

In real life, the magickal child is, in essence, all that comes from the union of Host and Hostess; including friends, family, unions, divisions, and even such seemingly material things that come with both wealth and poverty. In greater symbolism, the magickal child is all things that come from the union of Lord and Lady, the sum of this being life itself—the living world, if you will.

Magick and Rituals

In the case of magick, rituals are most often performed because like attracts like. That which one desires to manifest in life, one can do in ritual, hoping that like will attract like. This is one of the reasons the ancients practiced hunting before the actual hunt. (Forming a type of sacred theater, one would dress as the animal being hunted and the other hunters would symbolically chase and slay him.) From this, the ancients hoped that the ritual they had performed would create a pattern that the universe would follow in real life. Indeed, some of the most successful magick is started by first recognizing the groves (patterns) that already exist. This is why we tend to prefer ancient methods of effecting change over new methods, why runes are often preferred over the more recent alphabets.

In the past, I have respected the line that was drawn between religion and magick by Dr. Margaret Murray who essentially put forth the idea that there are two types of Witchcraft: Operational Witchcraft (which is better termed *spellcraft*) and Ritual Witchcraft (which is better termed *religious Witchcraft*). It is also important to point out that while it is possible to practice Operational Witchcraft (spellcraft) without religion, it is pointless to attempt to practice Ritual Witchcraft (religious) without its magickal aspects (spellcraft). If you do not believe this is the case, why then do we conduct our religious rituals?

Even in the simple celebration of life, there is magick. There is the affirmation that life is worthy of being celebrated, thus a conscious effort to influence our subconscious. That effort to cause change in the subconscious is in itself an effort toward creating the magickal child (the change).

Consider a harvest ritual. There is no need to work magick on the crops because they have already been taken in. The magick in a harvest rite can instead be found in the very fact that we celebrate a bountiful harvest. It provides us with the memories of what happens when the harvest is good. Those memories will carry into the next planting season, thus giving us further motivation for another successful harvest.

As part of their Yule celebration, many Wiccans greet the returning sun with an all-night drum circle. The circle ends when the sun is said to have been successfully drummed up. One might argue that we do not really believe the sun will not rise without our drum beat, but the magick here is not the action of causing the sun to rise. The magick is to cause doubt to set. The sun represents the light of our soul, so right in the middle of the darkest (longest) night, we drum to return the light to our soul.

We drum up the sun at Winter Solstice (Yule) because it is the shortest day of the year. With the dwindling light, so does our spirit dwindle as the year turns dark. Who can deny that Winter is the season with the highest suicide rate? So we drum up the sun and make other forms of merriment to keep our soul from slipping back into the dark place that I spoke of in the first chapter. No higher aspiration can one have for magick than the preservation of life and the potential for love. So we find the basic foundation of Wiccan ritual in just that; the preservation of life and the potential for love.

Some religions teach that sex causes karma, and karma is what causes one to be forever reincarnated. Of course it does. After all, if no one had sex, there would be no children into which we could reincarnate. Fortunately, Wicca is not one of those religions. With the understanding of the symbolism behind our rites, Wicca is rather open in the idea that sexual union is what has preserved humanity these many years.

The foundation of Wiccan ritual is sacred theater, which proclaims life is good. It is a celebration of the unions that form in love, and the fruit of those unions. In that respect, I do not feel our rites should be solemn. Oh, I am sure there is a time and place for such things, but even in a funeral rite, is it not better to dance for our lost loved ones than to cry? Wouldn't they prefer to see us happy, knowing that, although we do miss them, we will celebrate their lives rather than wallow in their deaths? I, for one, would prefer my death be marked with a wake rather than a funeral. Bury my ashes under an apple tree so you can eat my fruit every year and say, "A.J. is tasting good this year." Unfortunately, I think my friends might plant a Granny Smith.[1]

Thus, all of our rites mostly follow the same pattern in their beginning and ending. The middle is where they change to suit specific intentions, such as harvest rites, the working of additional magick, marking of the wheel of life, or rites of passage. The opening and closing can be conducted with a light heart, as I prefer, or solemnly, but their symbolism does not change, nor does the message given: Life is good. To get that message across, we celebrate life with the symbolism of creating life. Think of it as two lovers courting, becoming wed, consummating their union, and then parting with the hopes of coming together again.

Thus the debate between holding our rites solemnly or with a zest for life is akin to the choice between making love as the Christian Church once told Europe it should: without foreplay, in the missionary position, at night with the drapes closed, and only for procreation; or as uninhibited lovers do, with the zest of life itself. I say better we make love and ritual in a manner that, well, that all in attendance will enjoy.

With that vision, the basics of our rites can be transformed into many different rituals, but in each, they tell the story of beginning, middle, and end—birth, life and death:

Birth (The Beginning): The first date, the date itself, and the end of the date, with the promise that, if so willed, the couple will date again.

Life (The Middle): The start of the marriage ceremony, the consummation of the vows, and the ending of the ceremony, with the promise that, if willed, the bride and groom will come together again and again.

Death (The End): The start of a marriage, the marriage itself, and, when life has become short, that, if so willed, the couple will meet again in the next life.

Wiccan Ritual: Lustral Bath
Real Life: Personal Hygiene

If you have ever attended a public circle, chances are, you have had cause to think that the lustral bath has been forgotten by a few members of our religion. Indeed, in some of the public circles I have attended, one might think participants had forgone bathing entirely. Personal hygiene aside, the lustral bath serves to visualize intent, but this doesn't mean you should just *visualize* the water. The lustral bath is a very real emerging in and cleansing by water (and hopefully soap), usually in a bathtub, just prior to ritual. If you really want to do it right, I suggest a shower prior to the lustral bath to cleanse the body, and then a long soak to cleanse the mind and soul.

Here we all find our first ritual challenge. Did you know that practically all commercial soap is made with animal fat? Manufacturers hide it with words like *tallow* (processed fat from cattle, sheep, and horses). You may not be a vegetarian, but before using commercial soap prior to a lustral bath, ask yourself if you think it is appropriate to smear a product produced by death on your body before celebrating life? Instead, why not use castile soap, which is made from olive oil?

In this department, I have been very fortunate. In Chapter 2, I mentioned a friend who worked as a professional dominatrix. Well, she changed occupation and now makes some of the world's best animal-free soaps. (We like to say that she cleaned up her act.) If you are not fortunate enough to have a local soap creator of high caliber, check out her Website at *www.botanicalbaths.com*.

The lustral bath itself should not involve soap of any kind, because anything you add to your bath water is likely to remain on your body well into the ritual. Unless you are absolutely sure of every ingredient, it is easy to accidentally bring in elements that are counterproductive to the ritual's intent. Instead, let the lustral bath contain only influences you deliberately added.

Feel free to be creative. Most purists will tell you that a lustral bath contains nothing but water and sea salt, but adding to the mix can enhance your mood and help focus on the intent of the rite.[2] If the ritual has a specific purpose, adding herbs and oils in line with that intent is typically a good idea. Of course do so only within safety guidelines and in recognition of personal allergies.

In the case of a Host and Hostess who have already been initiated to each other (sexually active with each other), it can greatly heighten a rite if the lustral bath is enjoyed together. However, there are downsides to this practice. First, most tubs simply are not large enough. Second, you might have to fight over whose back is to the faucet (ouch). Finally, it might be too tempting to speed things right along to the Great Rite.

Wiccan Ritual: Dress With Intent
Real Life: Your Appearance Speaks a Lot About Who You Are.

As the host of the main ritual at the Real Witches Ball, I can tell you for a fact that the Pagan community has not yet established a dress code. This is a good thing. I can also tell you that as a whole, we have also not yet established common sense. This might not be such a good thing. In all fairness, we do have a very diverse attendance. Many of our guests come from much warmer climates, and I still have a bit of a chuckle when I see short pants worn at an October event in Ohio. When it comes to ritual, the key to knowing how to dress appropriately is just to remember that Wiccan rituals are social occasions. From there, you decide what is appropriate the way you would decide what is appropriate for any social function: by asking and by using common sense.

Even if your rite is to be conducted skyclad (naked), you should put consideration towards the cloths you will wear on your way to the ritual. Robes might seem traditional, but truth be known, the ancients dressed for ritual very much the way we dress for any social event—with everyday clothing when everyday clothing was called for, and with their finest when their finest was called for. Sure, that might have meant fancy robes back in the day, but what was appropriate back in the day might not be appropriate today (especially if you use public transportation).

In the case of a Host and Hostess who are already initiated to each other, it might seem tempting to enter the rite skyclad. However, even in the case where the actual Great Rite is the intent, disrobing each other is not only incredibly romantic, it makes for a great statement of consent just prior to the Great Rite (should it be performed rather than the symbolic Great Rite).

Wiccan Ritual: Preparing the Temple
Real Life: Making Your Home Presentable

The first real-life consideration in this act is where to place the home. Of course, considerations such as employment enter into this decision, but that should not be the only consideration. If you hope to have family and friends for holiday dinner, it is a good idea to look for a home close to your family and friends.

The next step in preparing the temple is in determining where it will be. This may change with the season and the rite, but it should always be both accessible and welcoming to your guests. If it is outdoors, make sure there are no logs, rocks, or holes on which your guests might trip. If the number of obstacles is too great, find a different location.

The next step is in cleansing the temple. One of my favorite visualizations for this is to use a broom (besom) to physically sweep the area in which circle will be held. Starting at the center, sweep your way out of the circle in a spiral while moving in the direction of banishing (counterclockwise). While sweeping the physical dust and gravel from a location, visualize negative energy being swept away with the dirt. Attaching small bells to your broom lets it do double duty, as bells have been historically used to ward off destructive forces. Smudging and asperges also work great (I will explain these in the next section).

Another real-life consideration here is making your home inviting to guests. If we believe like attracts like, then we really need to take a good, long look at our homes before ever thinking about raising our temple. I remember when I was a guest in the home of the president of a certain Pagan organization. The only thing more sickening than the stench of cat urine was the amount of fecal material on the floor in the room used as an office for that organization. If that person is reading this, let me say that even if your favorite Goddess form is Bast, cat feces just isn't very inviting.

In the case of a Host and Hostess who are already initiated to each other, this might be the act of arranging for a relative or babysitter to take your children elsewhere. It might be the act of drawing the drapes to keep out prying eyes, disconnecting the telephone, or even making plans for a vacation where no one will ever find you. Trust me on this last one. It is especially important if this is a handfasting ceremony, as there seems to be a tradition in the Pagan community in which kith and kin track down the groom and bride to torment them on their wedding night. Indeed, I think the tradition of tying tin cans to the bumper of the newlyweds' car might be an old tradition performed to help tormenters track their movements by sound.[3]

Wiccan Ritual: Smudging and Asperging
Real Life: Putting Guests at Ease

The acts of smudging and asperging can be used to cleanse locations, people, and objects. In the case of locations, the customs lend themselves well to the preparing of the temple. In the case of objects, these customs are used much the same. When it comes to people, it is entirely different. Unlike objects and locations, people have independent thought. No matter how much you urge them to leave negative energy at home, they tend to track it in unknowingly.

Smudging: Sage smoke is wonderful for this ritual, and sage bundles (smudge sticks) are available in just about every metaphysical store, as well as some herb shops. Additionally, some incenses have a very relaxing effect. Frankincense, dragon's blood, and copal are my favorites, as they seem to set the mood just right for the imagery and symbolism that I find in Wiccan rituals.

Asperging: This is a sprinkling of the location and people with holy water. It is in the preparation of that holy water that we find the first symbolism of sexual union, so don't run out to a Catholic church to get the water. Instead make your own. Into a chalice of water (representing the womb), measure three times what sea salt will fit on the tip of your athame. After the third measure, lower the athame into the chalice (representing the union of Lord and Lady). Stir (giving some pleasure and thus a light heart to it). This is best accomplished when the Hostess holds the chalice and the Host holds the athame.

Wiccan Ritual: Offering the Challenge and Banishing the Outsiders

Real Life: Insuring Consent

It is important to note that some folks prefer to offer the challenge prior to casting the circle. Others prefer to offer the challenge as a part of casting the circle. In the latter, the challenge is issued just before the circle is complete. Either way, at the risk of being called Wicca's next dictator, I say the challenge should be an important part of every Wiccan ritual, because it prompts an assurance of consent. Without it, we cannot be sure if those in attendance are present to participate in the rite or are there as spectators.

I also think it is a good idea to incorporate the outsiders into the challenge. I believe this ritual idea originated in the liturgy of the ADF. In essence, it is a reminder that we all bring things with us that we do not want in either the circle or in our lives. The outsiders are those who challenged the Creator (love) and lost. If we incorporate their banishment into our rite, then that rite will go a long way toward banishing them from our hearts.

A Public Samhain Challenge Example: "We are here to celebrate life and the lives of those who have come before. If you wish to partake of this rite, please stay for the casting of the circle, but then do not leave until the circle is open. If you wish to observe but not participate, please take 10 steps backward, and do not enter our circle until we have declared it open."

A Public Outsiders Example: "Let also leave the outsiders. Those who have challenged our Lord and Lady and lost. Those who are themselves greed, jealousy, bigotry, and all of those things that remain in our hearts although we fight them."

The outsiders are sometimes banished with much more than words. Sometimes people are asked to write on a piece of paper their own personal outsiders. Those pages are then collected and burned. Other times, the papers are handed to the Host and Hostess who toss them outside of the circle, lock them in a box, or otherwise offer a physical visualization for their removal.

In its respect to courting, the public rite can be seen as a group date. There are both those who are involved (as is the case with double dating) and those who are not involved (the friend who wants to tag along or the person who sells the movie tickets). In the case of the person who sells you the movie tickets, their 10 steps backward is normally understood, but the challenge is often very necessary for the friend who wants to tag along.

If the rite is private, the challenge should politely ask anyone who is not a participant to leave. Although you might not think the challenge is necessary in such situations, reality has shown us that, for some strange reason, many Pagans seem to feel that all rites are open to the public. In its respect to courting, the private rite can be seen as "alone time."

In both private and public matters, the challenge and in-suring of consent are not only between the couple and others in attendance, but between Host and Hostess as well. This is in the order of making sure each is on the same page. Is the date a romantic event, or two friends going out to see a movie? Better that each is aware of the other's intent for the evening up-front rather than suffer heartache later.

In the case of a Host and Hostess who are already initi-ated to each other, this step most certainly should not be over-looked in even the most personal and private of rites any more than should be the act of acquiring consent from a spouse prior to having sex. Rape is rape, married or not.

Here we find an interesting point when it comes to poly-amourous couples. A friend of mine was at a festival in Indiana with the five members of her polyamourous relationship. They were being rather free with their lovemaking in a rather public place when someone who was not a member of her polyam-ourous relationship joined in. Everyone was outraged. Although I do not see implied consent in their actions, I can certainly see how one might be confused, so better the challenge always be issued to make sure there is not failed communication as to who is in a circle or relationship before the rite or lovemaking begins.

Wiccan Ritual: Casting the Circle
Real Life: Building the Relationship/Building the Evening (a Circle Within a Circle)

The act of casting the circle can be likened to the building of a relationship. This is one of the many reasons I think the circle should be cast twice: once by the Host and once by the Hostess. The symbolism is that the union of the circle of family and friends of the Host and of the Hostess is one circle, a circle within a circle.

Typically, this is accomplished by going to the eastern-most part of the circle with an athame. Usually, the Host will point

an athame at the ground and visualize drawing energy from
Father Sky to unite with Mother Earth. In kind, the Hostess
will point an athame at the sky and visualize drawing energy
from Mother Earth to unite with Father Sky. Each walks clockwise one at a time or together from the eastern-most part of
the circle back to the eastern-most part of the circle.[4]

I say typically because there are definitely some traditions
that accomplish much the same in different ways. When we
consider the act of lovemaking, the ritual might be likened to
the simple act of closing the bedroom door. When we consider
handfasting, there are yet more ways (see Chapter 7). I think it
was Z. Budapest who suggested the circle be cast by tapping on
each wall of the home.

Wiccan Ritual: Inviting the Quarters
Real Life: Incorporating Family and
Friends into the Relationship

Just as the casting of the circle was the act of bringing the
Host and Hostess's circle of family and friends together, the
invitation to the Quarters symbolizes the interaction of these
two circles. Each Quarter has an associated Element, gender,
tool, and mate to each association.

Quarter	Element	Gender	Tool	Mate/Compliment
East	Air	Masculine	Censor	North, Earth, Female, Pentacle
South	Fire	Masculine	Athame	West, Water, Female, Chalice
West	Water	Female	Chalice	South, Fire, Masculine, Athame
North	Earth	Female	Pentacle	East, Air, Masculine, Censor

So we do not just call on the East Quarter to be present and watch over our rites. We call on the East Quarter to join our rites, by uniting it at center with the North Quarter (its mate). We do not just call on the South Quarter to be present and watch over our rites. We call on the South Quarter to join our rites, by uniting it at center with the West Quarter.

This recognizes that although Host and Hostess are a couple themselves, they would not be so if not for the couples that came before them (the Host's parents and the Hostess's parents). Arrange them as you please, while maintaining respect to the attributes and their relationships.

Primarily, these unions are:

Quarter	Symbolism
East	Hostess's Father
South	Host's Father
West	Host's Mother
North	Hostess's Mother

Alternatively, they can be:

Quarter	Symbolism
East	Host's Father
South	Hostess's Father
West	Hostess's Mother
North	Host's Mother

At the rite of handfasting, it is often desirable to mix these roles so that the Drawing of Quarters unites the Elements in a pattern that represents the union of the two families.

Quarters at the rite of handfasting:

Quarter	Symbolism
East	Hostess's Father
South	Host's Father
West	Hostess's Mother
North	Host's Mother

Alternatively, they can be:

Quarter	Symbolism
East	Host's Father
South	Hostess's Father
West	Host's Mother
North	Hostess's Mother

Typically, drawing or inviting the Quarters is accomplished by placing each Quarter's tool on a Quarter altar located at the edge of the circle in each of the four corresponding directions. East (Air) is most often called first, and then its mate, North (Earth). The censor is then taken from the Quarter altar at the East by a man, the pentacle is taken from the Quarter altar at the North, and the censor is placed on top of the pentacle in the center of the main altar (center circle). Next the South (Fire) and West (Water) and the athame and chalice (or sword and cauldron) are united.

As each element is both invited and united with its mate, words of intent based on the nature of the rite should be spoken. For example: In a cleansing rite, one might ask West Quarter to lend its energy to cleanse the circle. In that same rite, when West (Water) is united with South (Fire), one might ask the union to carry prayers as steam to return as a cleansing and nurturing rain. The same is true of the union of East (Air) with North (Earth).

Now, who hasn't had problems with their in-laws? This portion of our rite also reminds us that, although problems may well exist, those in-laws were necessary to bring forth the person whom you love.

Wicca Ritual: Invitation to Our Lord and Lady
Real Life: Proposal of Marriage

In most of the rituals I have attended, the invitation to our Lord and Lady takes the form of inviting them to be present in the rite. This is called *evoking* the Lord and Lady. Such invitations to our Lady are often given by the Hostess and to our Lord by Host.

Better our rites be in the order of *invoking* our Lord and Lady than *evoking* them. In so doing, we welcome them into our very being. Instead of simply inviting our Lord and Lady to witness our rites, better we invite them to participate in our rites as a bride would her groom at the wedding—inviting him to be her beloved. The Host invites his partner to become his Lady. In kind, the Hostess invites her partner to become her Lord.

If there are other couples in attendance, this is a good time to ask each to turn to their partners and do the same. It is also a good time to ask your guests to turn to each other and recognize that our Lord is present in all things male and our Lady in all things female, recognizing that even their neighbors are the earthly representatives of that which we praise.

Wiccan Ritual: The Symbolic Great Rite
Real Life: Consummation of Marriage

The symbolic Great Rite usually takes the form of lowering an athame into a chalice of wine[5] and speaking a few words: "As man is to woman, so is the athame to chalice; their union blessing both." The wine is then shared with everyone in attendance as the fruit of their union.

This symbolic Great Rite represents the consummation of the Host and Hostess's union. It represents their sexual union; the wine, their magickal child. One could argue that such symbolism has no place in a world faced with over population, but the fruit of that union is not only children. Who can argue that the world is much easier to face with a partner with whom you have no secrets?

In the case of courtship between those who are not initiated to each other, the symbolic Great Rite can be the meal shared during a date.

Wiccan Ritual: The Body of the Ritual
Real Life: The Life of the Couple

The body of the ritual is the reason for that ritual. It is the season or event that is being celebrated or what spellcraft is being performed. This is the life of the couple and their interaction with the greater community. This is the celebration (ritual) of a new job (life); it is the rite of passage (ritual) that marks a child's assent to adulthood (life); and it is all aspects of the life shared by the Host, Hostess, and all of the circles within circles, comprised of their friends and family. It is also the hard times that couples will face, and the challenge to find ways of overcoming obstacles with spellcraft (ritual) and the hard work that is often necessary to find success in spellcraft (life).

Wiccan Ritual: Thanking the Lord and Lady
Real Life: Thanking Your Partner

In this ritual, we see an excellent reason to *invoke* our Lord and Lady rather than *evoke* them. If you have invited your partner to be your Lord or Lady, as was suggested earlier, this parting can be a wonderful time to assure them of their continued freedom. It is a time to affirm that love binds with the heart rather than with chains or rope.

> Host speaks to Hostess: "Thank you for being my Lady in this rite and in my life. Stay if you will, but go if you must."

The Hostess can then assure the Host of his freedom in kind.

Wiccan Ritual: Thanking the Quarters
Real Life: The Party Is Over

As was the thanking of the Lord and Lady, this is a chance for friends and family to assure each other that they, too, are bound by love, not by chains. And that even as the couple who brought them together has parted, the choice to remain united for friends and family is also still a matter of the heart. In ritual, this often involves returning the tools to the Quarter altars.

Wiccan Ritual: Walking Down and Opening the Circle
Real Life: The Act of Handparting

In most cases, I feel it is a good idea to *walk down* the circle (uncast it). This is done much the way the casting of the circle was done, except that it is done counterclockwise. However, in the case of a handparting rite, better not to walk down the circle. Instead, let the circle stand, and affirm to the guests that although many of them may have been brought together by this union, the circles of family and friends that the union formed cannot by this couple be unformed.

Whether walked down or not, the opening of the circle is the last part of the ritual. It is nothing formal; it just lets everyone know the circle is now open and they are free to enter and leave it as they will. In the case of a handparting, this is also the announcement that the couple is now open to new loves, who may present themselves as they will.

The Host's last words: "Merry did we meet."

The Hostess's last words: "Merry do we part."

Everyone in attendance responds: "And merry will we meet again."

So, in ritual it is as in life, three stages of union: the beginning, the middle, and the end. It is interesting to note that the rite of handfasting in most traditions involves the dedication of a year and a day (roughly 13 moons). In our basic ritual format, we also see the number 13, here as the number of steps involved in the basic ritual format.

➤ **The Beginning: The First Date (the Maiden and Master state of union)**

 1. Lustral bath: Removing the dirt and grime that you do not want on your date.

2. Dress: Be appropriately outfitted for the nature of the date. T-shirts won't do at a black-tie affair.

3. Preparing the temple: Selecting where the date will take place, insuring it is appropriate to the evening and nature of the date.

4. Smudging and asperging: Helping your date to be at ease with you, holding the door, bringing a gift, complementing each other's choice of outfits.

5. Offering the challenge: Ensuring the nature of the date.

6. Casting the circle: Beginning the relationship with the first date.

7. Inviting the Quarters: Giving respect to the parents (bring flowers for mom, too).

8. Inviting the Lord and Lady: Exploring the idea that there will be a second date.

9. Symbolic Great Rite: Consuming a meal.

10. Body of the Ritual: Getting to know each other, watching a video or movie to see what causes your date to laugh or cry.

11. Thanking Lord and Lady: Thanking your date for the time you have spent together.

12. Thanking the Quarters: Letting your date know that you are very happy that family and friends brought you together.

13. Walking down and opening the circle: Concluding the date by asking for another date, or deciding and communicating the idea that one will or will not call. Better to be honest that friends who might have been lovers remain friends rather than become enemies.

➢ **The Middle: Marriage (the Mother and Father state of union)**

1. Lustral bath: Removing the dirt and grime that you do not want in your wedding.

2. Dress: What type of wedding is it? Traditional formal and medieval can both be beautiful, but don't always mix well.

3. Preparing the temple: Selecting the location of the ceremony. Shall it be in your home, a state park, or maybe, by a parent's insistence, a mosque, temple, or church? Remember: Muslim, Jew, or Christian, our law is such that the Creator (by any name) is love, so the Creator's home by any name is a house of love.

4. Smudging and asperging: Efforts to make everyone comfortable in your rite. This might involve burning a relaxing incense.

5. Offering the challenge: This may be asking guests to bless the union, or—if you want to risk it—asking that if they do not speak against it now, to forever offer such blessing of silence.

6. Casting the circle: The ceremony begins.

7. Inviting the Quarters: The bride's and groom's parents are welcomed. In western tradition, they are seated.

8. Inviting the Lord and Lady: The saying of "I do."

9. Symbolic Great Rite: Eating the cake, symbolizing mutual nourishing and the pending consummation of the union.

10. Body of the Ritual: The wedding reception.

11. Thanking Lord and Lady: Thanking your suitor for becoming your husband or wife.

12. Thanking the Quarters: Thanking the family and friends for attending and for bringing the couple together.

13. Walking down and opening the circle: Letting guests know that either the reception is over, or that it continues without the couple. The bride and groom are released from further social obligation to steal away to their honeymoon or wedding bed. Here we see the principle of being separated for the sake of union. In this case, they are separated from the trappings of ritual for union in real life (sex).

➤ **The End: Divorce and Death (the Crone and Sage State of Union)**

The rite of handparting is discussed in great detail in Chapter 10. I list it here only to preserve the representation of the three stages of life.

7 Handfasting and the Couple's Book of Shadows

Is Rosaline, that thou didst love so dear,
So soon forsaken? Young men's love then lies
Not truly in their hearts, but in their eyes.

—William Shakespeare, *Romeo and Juliet* 2.20

Introduction

One might think that among the great many books addressing a fertility religion, one could find many books that address the rites of handfastings and heartjoinings. But I know of only one. It was written by Lady Maeve Rhea and is appropriately titled *Handfasted and Heartjoined* (Citadel, 2001).

In this chapter, I do not seek to replace that book. In fact, if you wish to be joined to your love in the rite of handfasting, I encourage you to read it. But please also consult literature that might seem less Pagan in origin. This rite may well be the single-most important decision of your life, so please enter into it not only with the advice of fellow Pagans, but also with the secular advice of those who address the mundane issues facing a new bride and groom. Libraries, and of course book stores, have a wide variety of helpful books on subjects including dating, wedding etiquette, wedding planners, wedding showers, toasts, vows, ceremonies, and financial planning for newlyweds, just to name a few.

If you can only look to one place in Wicca to see the abuse of our law, look to the rite of handfasting. Once it was a sacred union between two souls. Today that which we call sacred is called upon for the slightest fancy, rather than as a committed union. Those calling for this sacred rite often tend to be little more than children playing with dolls, rather than adults carefully interweaving their hearts.

Here we must be guarded, and not grant consent to this rite for those without conviction. Love for those who would love, but commitment only for those who are willing to commit. To make this so, I say let four people stand and give consent before two may be wed. And better it be that these four be the mothers and fathers of those who would come to union in this manner. If the parents are not willing or available, then let it be two other couples who have been happily wed for many years. Like attracts like.

Handfasting

In my view of Wicca, there are three different rites of handfasting. In context of the greater community, these are equated to engagement, marriage, and a twilight promise. In relationship to the three stages of life, they are:

> ➤ Handfasting 1: Maiden and Master

> ➤ Handfasting 2: Mother and Father

> ➤ Handfasting 3: Crone and Sage

Some might argue that this view is too restrictive, that a couple needs time prior to a legally binding engagement to get to know each other. To this I agree, but say that this is not a handfasting but a courtship. Thus, we begin our discussion of handfasting at the sacred point when courtship asks for commitment.

For the purpose of discussion, I refer to one party of this partnership as the bride and one as the groom. In extension, I refer to the bride's parents and the groom's parents. However, I do so for the ease of discussion only. I neither exclude same-sex couples from this rite, nor do I imply that man being groom and woman being bride are not equal in this rite. Failing the parents' ability or willingness to participate, friends can most certainly stand in for them. Assign these titles as they fit your own needs and desires.

The First Handfasting—Engagement

Best During a New or Waxing Moon of Spring

The first rite of handfasting is engagement. As such, it should be treated with as much reverence, respect, and (dare I say) conviction. This is a trial period, a time when potential groom and potential bride shall live as they intend to once wed. This is most certainly not the more traditional engagement when two become dedicated but live during this period celibate and apart. Thus, it should be entered into with as much dedication as the second handfasting (legal marriage), and not lightly, as might be the case in courting.

One might argue that we should not insist that a couple live as husband and wife during this rite, because it is not a legal marriage. To these folks, I ask that if that be the case, how then should one decide if a legal marriage should take place? Better we enter into commitment with eyes open, and better it be that a taste of what is to come, both sweet and bitter, be had prior the commitment (which can only be undone by the courts).

The terms of this union are as you have probably read elsewhere, but it is the longest of these two that is the commitment:

"A year and a day or for as long as love shall stay."

If the relationship should fail after six months, the bond is still in place for the remainder of the year and a day. If love should stay for years beyond, then so does the bond.

Now, as for the commitment: Let the words be said in the rite, but also written on paper and agreed to by both prior to the rite. These are the vows. Although such things are often frowned upon, they are also a prenuptial agreement. Where some might argue that this is preparing for divorce rather than celebrating union, I say that it is the Wiccan way to know that with life, there is death. The vows will become the first page of a couple's Book of Shadows.

The Second Handfasting: Marriage
Best during a Full Moon of Summer

The second rite of handfasting is that of marriage. As such, it should be treated with as much reverence, respect, and (dare I say) legality. If we are to demand the respect afforded to a legally recognized couple, then we should be ready to bear the same weight: that should the union fail, a fair and educated person should dissolve the contract if we cannot ourselves. That person would be a judge, and the act, a divorce.

In the case of same-sex couples, most governments do not yet afford set law for either marriage or divorce. Where the government forbids such unions, seek legal recognition as domestic partners.

In Chapter 4, I touched on the need for state-recognized Pagan clergy, but said that their role in the rite of handfasting should be nothing more than the role that might be played by a notary. With that view, we give respect to both heterosexual couples and homosexual couples. Let the state-recognized minister be included in the second rite of handfasting in the same role as the notary in the domestic partnership agreement of a same-sex couple.

The Third Handfasting: A Twilight Promise
Best During a Dark or Waning Moon of Fall[1]

Because Wiccans see life as a cycle of birth, life, and death, the final handfasting is best discussed along with the handparting (see chapter 10). I list it here only to preserve the representation of the three stages of life.

On the Issue of Union and Safe Sex

Now, I assure you that what I am about to say comes from intellect rather than heart, and much less, libido. Listen to this if you will, ignore it as I have many a time, but I count courtship as no less than six months of celibacy prior to the first handfasting. In the case of unions larger than two, I say the same. When courting a new partner, that potential partner should be celibate, and the polyamourous couple should, at a minimum, not have sex outside of their pre-existing union. Why?

1. As in all magick, the best release of tension is the point when the most energy is available. What better way to insure a memorable release than to abstain prior? Besides, this way there is a better chance you will remember the date you first had sex as a couple. Wouldn't that be a great thing to celebrate once a year?

2. An up-front agreement of abstinence will probably insure that a courtship is more of the heart than of the body. I, for one, know of no woman I could tolerate for six months if my intention were only sex. Thus this process weeds out sexual predators.

3. Six months of celibacy prior to screening for sexually transmitted disease greatly improves the accuracy of testing for such diseases.

Now, I am not saying that it is wrong, immoral, or unethical to have sex prior to handfasting. However, let that sex be clearly for the joy of it, such that there is no confusion as to intent. Thus, even if a couple is sexually active prior to considerations of handfasting, I still see the benefit in becoming celibate six months prior to that union. It seems true that if a sexually active couple can withstand such a test, they can withstand just about anything.

If you have trouble with abstaining, an oil to help in this goal is made by blending six drops of camphor oil with three drops of lavender oil into a base of coconut oil. Alternatively, you can carry a sachet containing one part natural camphor and three parts lavender flowers. With either oil or sachet, smell the mixture when you feel tempted, and with any luck, your desires will be decreased.

The Ritual: Jumping Sword and Broom

I wrote this some time ago for a friend who wanted her parents involved in her wedding, but knew that they would feel uncomfortable in a rite that was completely unfamiliar to them. So, I incorporated many themes found in more common weddings. Many will argue that this is not a traditional handfasting because essentially, I made it up. To those I ask: What is not made up?

The ritual for each part of handfasting should come from the heart more than from any book. In other words, you should "make up" your own rite. That said, I give you as example what I find in my own heart for the first two rites of handfasting (for the third rite, see Chapter 10).

Lustral Bath

Important considerations here include scent and taste. If this will be the first time you share each other's bodies, your haste after the formal rite might cause you to skip the lustral bath for your more private rite of initiation to each other. Best, then, you risk your body's natural odor than to risk placing deodorant, perfume, or anything else on your body that might be unpleasant to the tongue, if later you are to welcome that tongue on your body.

Pleasant and lust-inspiring herbs to use here include patchouli and sandalwood. There are other lust-inspiring herbs, but these seem best for bath. Grind the herbs and bundle in a cheese cloth to prevent from clogging the drain. Draw your bath as hot as possible, drop in this bundle, and let it steep until the water cools to a comfortable bathing temperature.

Dress

Oftentimes a bride will spend thousands of dollars on a wedding gown. However, she often devotes very little consideration for what her groom will see when it is removed. This is also the case with the groom and what his bride will see when his tuxedo is removed. Better we dress and undress to please our mates on this occasion than out of practicality.

You might think me insane for this idea, but it has been my observation that women's undergarments tend to be much more complicated than men's. It might be a good, yet sneaky and silly, idea for the bride to have her maid of honor (or like person) bring the bride's intended undergarments to the groom right in the middle of his bachelor party. Not only will this bring the groom's attention away from the stripper his friends may have hired, and back to his bride, but it will give him the chance to unlock the mysteries of his bride's undergarments. Yes, it is sneaky and silly, but isn't that the very nature of the nymphs chased by our Lord Pan?

Preparing the Temple

Although this is likened to choosing the location of the rite, the real-world consideration here is best left to the family and friends, such that the bride and groom not have another worry to distract them from the bliss that is to come.

Smudging and Asperging

This can be accomplished in the same way as any other rite. However, here it is pleasant to use incense appropriate to the union. Patchouli comes to mind because it imitates male pheromones, thus slightly elevating the pheromones in women. Back and forth it goes until the subtle scents of the room enhance the bride's and groom's appetite to share each other. Alternatively, try dragon's blood resin burned over charcoal.

If possible, have those who will stand at the Quarters arrange all the guests in a circle, explaining the traditional meaning of the circle as well as its association to the wedding ring. If the number of guests is too large for a circle, then arrange for a seating place for the majority of the guests, that they might witness but not participate in the rite.

Casting the Circle and Offering the Challenge

In the rite of handfasting, I think it best that the challenge be issued in conjunction with the casting of the circle as opposed to prior to it.

Starting at the eastern-most point of where the circle will be cast, the Flower Girls (Maidens) each stand with a basket of rose petals. Beside the Flower Maidens stand the Flower Boys (Masters) with baskets of patchouli. The bride stands outside of the circle, preferably where she cannot be seen. Those four who would stand at the Quarters do so. At the center of the circle stands the groom.

The rose petals are a symbol of our Lady and the Flower Maidens a symbol of youth. The patchouli herb is a symbol of our Lord and the Flower Masters a symbol of youth. Thus, we see here our Lord and Lady about to cast the circle in their aspect as Maiden and Master.

When all is ready, the groom rings a bell, opens the book containing the wedding vows, and lights a candle to announce the beginning of the rite. The playing of a light music to heighten moods just after the bell is rung is a good idea. Upon hearing the bell and the start of the music, the Flower Maidens and Masters walk clockwise, side by side, sprinkling the flowers outward to define the circle.

The Keep (minister, notary, or other witness) tells the guests of the symbolism behind the casting of the circle this way:

"The rose represents the bride and the patchouli her groom. Here we scatter them to the ground that they fall in union, patchouli and rose, groom and bride, bride and groom, thus establishing this circle as their new home entwined in each other's hearts and each other's arms."

The Flower Maidens and Masters stop just before closing the circle, thus leaving a few feet between where they started and where they ended. This is the gateway.

The Challenge Is Given and the Circle Is Closed

The Keep speaks:

"We are gathered here to mark the union of [bride's name] and [groom's name] as partners in all things that may come. The bitter and the sweet. Let none stand here but by consent and if that consent not be given, then speak words against this union and leave through this gate [point to the portion of the circle not yet closed] once your words are heard. [Pause appropriately.] Then let the bride and groom know union."

I know it sounds corny, but the "Bridal Chorus" (aka "Here Comes the Bride") will put everyone at further ease, as well as universally signal that the rite is about to begin. The bride, with her broom (besom), enters the circle through the gate. The Flower Maidens and Masters close the gate by sprinkling the bride with the patchouli and rose petals. The Flower Maidens and Masters then join the parents within the circle.

The bride places her besom at her groom's feet, symbolic of her role as woman (read that stereotype). Accepting that role, the groom picks up the broom and places it at the gate.

He returns to his bride and places his sword at her feet, symbolic of his role as man (read that stereotype). Accepting that role, the bride picks up the sword and places it with the broom (across the gate).

Inviting the Quarters

Air and Earth. Father of the groom stands at the East Quarter, representing the Element Air, and holds the censor (filled with burning incense). Mother of the bride stands at the North Quarter, representing the Element Earth, and holds the pentacle.

The groom asks the mother of the bride: "Will you bring your blessings to this union?"

The bride asks the father of the groom: "Will you bring your blessings to this union?"

The mother of the bride and father of the groom bring their tools to the center altar. The pentacle is placed on the altar and then the censor on top of that. The mother of the bride and father of the groom then welcome the merging of the families in their own words, and then embrace.

Fire and Water. Father of the bride stands at the South Quarter, representing the Element Fire, and holds the athame. Mother of the groom stands at the West Quarter, representing the Element Water and holds a chalice (filled with water).

The groom asks his mother: "Will you bring your blessings to this union?"

The bride asks her father: "Will you bring your blessings to this union?"

The father of the bride and mother of the groom bring their tools to the center altar. The athame is lowered into the chalice, there is a pause, and then the two tools are separated and placed on the altar. The father of the bride and mother of the groom then welcome the merging of the families in their own words, and then embrace.

Inviting the Lord and Lady

It doesn't matter who goes first. Flip a coin and call the selection divine if you must. The invitation to the Lord and Lady is in the order of reading the vows (agreed upon earlier) and then asking each other: Do you agree to this covenant?

Groom asks bride: "Do you agree to [read vows]?"

In answer, the bride lights a pink candle (preferably of the type used to seal envelopes) and drips its hot wax onto the written vows stating, "I do."

Bride asks groom: "Do you agree to [read vows]?"

In answer, the groom lights a red candle (preferably of the type used to seal envelopes) and drips its hot wax next to hers that they remain separate but also intertwine. He says, "I do."

The bride and groom join hands (bride's left with groom's right). The Keep or any other useful person lightly ties their hands with a soft cord to symbolize their union.

Together bride and groom (husband and wife) speak: "Then by the power invested in us by the law that is love, we pronounce ourselves as husband and wife." If this is a legal wedding, the Keep can announce much the same of the law that he or she brings.

The Symbolic Great Rite

The first kiss shared as husband and wife can be the symbolic Great Rite here. However, if so choosing, the couple can leap the broom and sword at this point and let the first part of the reception go on without them while they engage in another symbolic form of the Great Rite (remember, the actual great rite is of the heart and not the body). That decision should probably be made of the moment rather than being planned. If they choose to leave, let the circle stand and have them leap both sword and broom.

The symbolism here is that, although they came together as man and woman (with all the traditional stereotypes), they leap those stereotypes as a couple, thus forming a shared role.

Body of the Ritual

In a handfasting, the body of the ritual is as the wedding reception is: a celebration of the union that has taken place. If your gathering is small, you can open a gate in the circle (remove sword and broom) for people to come and go. If that is the case, the revelry can be conducted in circle. But in groups of any size, it is probably best to move to open the circle and commence the reception when it is easier to come and go (as well as sit and eat).

Thanking the Lord and Lady

If husband and wife are still present, the thanking of the Lord and Lady should be in the format of thanking each other for their union and reminding each other that although bound by love they are free by will.

If the husband and wife have stolen off, the thanking of the Lord and Lady can be done by the father of the groom and mother of the bride.

Thanking the Quarters

The thanking of the Quarters should be done by those who invited them, as in any other Wiccan rite. However, let their thanks also be in the act of thanking each other, not only for their participation in the rite, but for their participation in the lives of the two who have been united.

Opening the Circle

A bell is rung indicating the ending of the rite. The book in which the wedding vows were written is closed and the candle that was lit when the rite began is extinguished.[2]

Someone speaks, "The bell has rung, the book is closed, and the candle is extinguished. Merry did we meet. Merry do we part."

Guests reply: "And merry will we meet again."

A Couple's Book of Shadows

In the time when covens outnumbered solitary practitioners, each coven was said to have its own Book of Shadows. Out of that Book of Shadows, members would copy portions for their own book. As Wicca became more focused on the solitary practitioner, a Book of Shadows changed into more of a personal journal. Material for those personal journals is often copied from published works.

When it comes to a handfasted couple, let each keep a personal Book of Shadows if they will, but let also the union keep its own book from the time of their first handfasting. Think of it as a wedding album that grows with time. As such, let the first entrance into this Couple's Book of Shadows be the vows from the first handfasting and the last be the vows of the final handfasting (either death vows or divorce). Let the book then remain with the survivor until such time as they leave this world, then unto their children, that their union serve as example for generations to come. In the case of divorce, let the book be destroyed, thus it not haunt either parted member.

8   Spellcraft and Rituals for Couples

Man masters nature
not by force but by understanding.
This is why science has succeeded
where magic failed:
because it has looked for no spell to
cast over nature.

—Jacob Bronowski

Introduction

At the Real Witches Ball 2001, one of the many workshops was led by Laurie Kelly from New Page Books, the publisher of this very book. The workshop was basically a question-and-answer session asking, "What do you, the Pagan community, want to see in print?" The general consensus from the attendees was that the Pagan community is sick and tired of "spellbooks" and other similar collections of what authors claim to have worked. Instead, they seemed to want sensible literature aimed at the spirituality behind our religion rather than the spells. I could see the smile on Laurie's face as she left the workshop, confident that she could return to her publisher with the news that the Pagan community had grown up. Unfortunately, that image of the Pagan community as a whole may be only skin deep.

A few hours later, another workshop featured Dorothy Morrison. That workshop was based on Dorothy's book *Everyday Magic*, and was basically a presentation around the book's subtitle, "Spells & Rituals for Modern Living." Now I absolutely adore Dorothy Morrison. In fact, I am comfortable using the word love to describe how I feel about her, but as I've said, *Everyday Magic* is not one of my favorite books by her pen. It very well may be the absolute finest spellbook, but that genre is most certainly not my favorite. Attending that workshop were most of the same people who attended Laurie's workshop, and then some. So many, in fact, that the workshop was just about standing room only. Observing this workshop, it became clear what was under the skin.

Indeed, it has become politically correct to say that we are sick and tired of spellbooks. Although I usually have a knee-jerk reaction to most things PC, I feel some sense of pride knowing I have been at least partially responsible for nudging the Pagan community in that direction. However, there is still a very long way to go before our spellcraft and rituals regain their sacred role in the everyday lives of Wiccans and other modern Pagans. We have started talking the talk, but now we have to walk the walk. Publishers publish what will sell. If we want them to publish material that addresses the heart and soul of our religion, then we are duty-bound to show our desire in what we do and do not purchase.

So why include a chapter on spellcraft at all? Because spellcraft is an important part of both our religion and the relationships that we form. Note that I said "spellcraft" and not just "spells." You see, when it comes to couples, spellcraft is to spells as the decision-making process is to the decision. Simply yanking someone else's spells out of a book might be effective, but not personal. Spellcraft is like the relationship itself: mostly exploration. With that in mind, please consider what follows to be more of examples, suggestions, and theory provided to help you build your own spells through your personal involvement in the art that is spellcraft.

Science succeeds where magick has failed because science is nothing more than magick that has been understood. You see, understanding is the first step towards mastery. However, the greatest force the universe will ever know is something that the universe will never fully understand: love. Thus, when it comes to matters of the heart, there can be no science. Fortunately, even without hard science, we still have spellcraft and rituals that seem to work, even though we do not fully understand why.

Spellcraft for couples is a combination of the seemingly explained (soft science) and the seemingly unexplained (magick) stirred together gently with what we will never fully understand (love). In other words, much of what you are about to read might seem to fall under the S.W.A.G. category (Scientific Wild Ass Guess).

Now that might make you think I don't have much faith in spellcraft. But note that the term begins with the word *scientific*. Although we will probably never fully understand love enough to call our understanding science, we can definitely use the scientific method to improve what knowledge we do have. (See Chapter 1 of *Wicca Spellcraft for Men* for my views on spellcraft and the scientific method.)

Home Blessing: Making the Home Ready for Both Magick and Mundane

One of the main thoughts I hope this book will change in the Wiccan community is our idea of the temple, commonly thought to be circle. It is actually the home. The circle itself is only a symbol of that home in the way the symbolic Great Rite is only a symbol of the union of souls. I can think of no better way to illustrate this than with a home blessing.

Lustral Bath

The home blessing is a wonderful opportunity to incorporate romance and, dare I say it, sex into Wiccan ritual. To build energy, the lustral bath can be shared. If your tub isn't large enough, take turns gently bathing each other.

Dress

What will your neighbors think if you dance around your yard naked or clad in those stereotypical black robes? Good neighbors, hopefully, will take notice. Why are these good neighbors? Well, those same neighbors are going to call the police when something suspicious is happening while you are away. In time, you may hope to develop a trusting relationship with them and conversation may move towards religion. The home blessing is not that time. Dressing as one would for yard work seems in order.

Preparing the Temple

Of course a great deal of though has gone into selecting and purchasing a new home. But for the purpose of this ritual, you will need a magickal tool that seems missing from most Wiccans' collections of ritual tools, the compass. Most homes are either square or rectangular, so this step will be easy. If you have an irregularly shaped home, just do your best. Use the compass to determine how your home is situated in respect to the four directions. Chances are, either one wall or corner will face each direction. If you want to map it out on paper, this is a great addition to the couple's Book of Shadows.

Smudging and Asperging

Take turn smudging and asperging each other, then decide who will do which and walk a circle around your home bathing it lightly in smoke and salted water. If the neighbors ask and you prefer to gradually acquaint them to your spirituality, you can always tell them it is a Native American tradition for blessing the home without lying. If they are out and about, you might even want to introduce yourself to them and explain that it might look a bit strange but it is appropriate.

Offering the Challenge

This can be in the order of couples asking each other if they are ready to make love in their new home for the first time and assuring each other that they have brought no baggage (outsiders) from former relationships into the new home.

Casting the Circle

Starting at the eastern-most wall or corner as determined when you prepared the temple, walk clockwise hand in hand until you arrive at the starting point.

Inviting the Quarters

Standing at the eastern-most point in your circle, plant, erect, bury, or place an item that is associated with that Quarter to watch over your home. The more effort you put towards researching, selecting, and/or making these items together, the better it will serve to further the act of discovering each other. After a Quarter is invited in this way, walk clockwise to the next Quarter and do the same. After your invitation to the North Quarter, continue to walk clockwise until you arrive at the front door of your home.

Invitation to the Lord and Lady

This is in the order of inviting your partner into your home for the first time. If you want to do the traditional and still very romantic—man carries woman over the threshold—that is great! But be sure to come up with a balancing symbolic gesture that makes it clear that both are invited and none forced.

Great Rite

What better time and place to make love?

Body of the Ritual

Preparing the home both magickally and mundanely. Perhaps you will want to place tiger's eye in the corners of the home for protection, or aventurine in the corners of the home office for prosperity. Unpacking and placing images of fertility Gods and Goddesses in the bedroom is a good idea at this point if you desire children. Then there is the mundane unpacking and cleaning that both can become magickal acts when you incorporate them into this rite, making moving in not only fun, but sacred.

Thanking the Lord and Lady

After you finish the unpacking and setting up your new home, thank each other for participating in the rite and the home.

Thanking the Quarters

Still within the home, go to the walls or corners of each Quarter as determined earlier and thank not only the Quarter, but the wall or corner itself. Essentially, you are thanking not only the forces that watch over you home, but the structure of the home itself for making itself available. As time goes by, you will begin to think of your home as part of the relationship itself.

Opening the Circle

Instead of formally opening the circle by walking it down, consider the opening of the circle to be opening your home to guests. This is the point where both agree that the rite of blessing the home was complete and the home is ready to serve as both a gathering place for kith and kin and the center of the magick that you will work together.

The Home Is Where the Spells Are Cast

Some books will tell you that all Wiccan magick must be practiced within a cast circle. I believe this is held over from our perception of the Burning Times, like black robes and secret meetings. The Wiccan temple was probably thought to be a cast circle because it is portable. If one location was discovered, the coven could simply cast another at a different location. On the other hand, Gardner and others may have included it in Wicca after borrowing it from medieval ceremonial magick. If so, it is unfortunate, because not much thought was given to the differences between the celebrations of pre-Christian fertility religions and medieval ceremonial magicians.

Consider the harvest festival. Are we expected to believe that a grand feast was held within the confines of a 9-foot circle on the ground? And what of larger groups? Painstaking experimentation has shown that casting a circle around a circle of, let's say a thousand people, robs a great deal of the crowd's energy and anticipation. I think such circles are best reserved for rituals where the casting of the circle is an intricate part of the rite itself. Examples of this involvement can be found in the rites I have included in the chapters on handfasting, hand-parting, and Wiccaning.

Other than those rites and other times when the casting of the circle is part of the ritual itself, once the home is blessed in a way similar to the above rite, spells and rituals conducted within it are as spells and rituals conducted within a cast circle. After all, the cast circle represents the home, but within its walls your rites are conducted within the real thing. It is a good idea to repeat this or similar home blessings for each Sabbat and High Day, if not for its magickal benefits, then to remind the homeowners of the sanctity of the home. Of course, if the particular celebration involves other folks, you will probably want to substitute the symbolic Great Rite of lovemaking, with a kiss shared by Host and Hostess.

Thus, because the blessed home is the circle itself, it is not necessary to cast additional circles. This greatly increases the activity that can take place within the Wiccan circle, allowing us to incorporate cooking, eating meals, and other festivities that typically do not fit into the confines of a one-room circle.

Home Protection

Once the home has been blessed, one of the first bits of spellcraft a couple will probably want to do is to protect the home from negative energy. Wards, plaques, and other symbols of protection are as old as recorded history and can be incorporated into not only protection for the home but protection for the relationship inside the home.

These wards are typically out in the open, so it is a good idea to make them both attractive and unthreatening. After all, if you were to lob off an enemy's head and place it on a pole in your front yard as the Celts once did, you'd probably have a hard time getting someone to deliver your mail, much less install cable television. So find a time when both of you can go shopping for craft supplies and set aside an afternoon to chat over the kitchen table as you prepare to ward off all the things that might go bump in the night.

Mirrors

Mirrors have been used as wards for almost as long as they have been available. Today, they can be found in a variety of shapes and sizes. One-foot square mirror tiles are usually available at the hardware store for less than $2 each, but will require a glass cutter and probably a bit of skill with stained glass for our purposes here. So if you have the tools and the skills, you will quickly understand how to use them to create a much more attractive version of this simple ward. If, however, you do not have those tools and skills, read along. The instructions are simple.

Small round mirrors no larger than the top of a soda can are relatively easy to find. On a piece of newspaper on a table, lay out half the mirrors in a line face down. In the center of each mirror in the line, place a few drops of epoxy (white glue will work in a pinch). Place a ribbon in the glue (you'll use this to hang the mirrors). Place another dab of epoxy on top of the ribbon, and finally add another mirror on top so you have a sandwich where the mirrors are the bread and the ribbon is the middle. Let the glue dry well, then hang the mirrors by the ribbon.

Witches Bottles

If you should happen to break a mirror you had intended to use as a ward, don't worry about the bad luck. Chances are that's a leftover bit of lore from when mirrors cost a great deal. Just go on with your plans to use the mirror as a ward, but instead, set the broken bits aside to use in the making of a Witches Bottle. Almost anything will do for this bottle, but make sure the mouth is wide (large mason jars work well). If you should happen to break plates, bowls, or glasses, they will work too. Additionally, if you have prickly or thorny brush that you want to remove from your property, save a few of the branches or thorns for the Witches Bottle. Make it a game to find sharp things in your home and yard that have no purpose beyond harming the foot or a tire. Rusty nails are ideal. Place what you can find in your bottle.

If along the way you should happen to cut yourself by accident, allow the blood to drip into the bottle, but never intentionally harm yourself. Traditionally menstrual blood and urine have been used in the bottle. Their inclusion should be by choice only; it is not mandatory.

Fill the rest of the bottle with rain water. Collect it by standing in a downpour, each holding the bottle. Finally, secure the top and put in a safe place where the bottle will not be touched. You might want to bury one on either side of your driveway, or perhaps in the four Quarters of your property line. Be aware that this mixture will build up enough pressure to eventually burst the glass. The more sunlight it receives, the sooner it will burst.

Witches Balls

Most Witches Balls are handmade by blowing glass of many colors into a hollow ball with a hole at one end. The balls are thought to trap negative energy. They are beautiful, and according to many, very functional. They are usually hard to make and expensive. But I've figured out an easy and affordable way to make them.

Most craft stores sell clear glass Yule ornaments (best to ask for Christmas ornaments). They are thin glass balls with a hole on top for the ring by which they are hung. They also sell bake-on glass paint that can be fused in your own oven at very low temperatures. Purchase an assortment of balls and paint, and spend an evening making Witches Balls with your partner to protect your home. These also make wonderful gifts during the holiday season.

Remove the metal cap from the ball and set it aside. Take turns decorating the inside or the outside of the ball with spots of color. If you want to define the different areas of color as if it were made of stained glass, you can also use a product sometimes called liquid led. When you are finished, follow the directions on the paint for baking time and temperature.

After your Witches Ball has cooled, decide if it is going to be given as a Yule/Christmas gift or a Witches Ball. If it is going to be used as a gift for the holidays, simply reinsert the metal cap and you have a handmade ornament. If you are going to use it as a Witches Ball, point the opening to one side and epoxy (glue won't work) the cap onto the top of the ball such that when you hang it, the opening will be to the side. Witches Balls are generally hung in windows, especially around the front and back doors.

Keeping the Outsiders Outside

In our rituals, we often include the act of banishing or sometimes appeasing the outsiders—the forces that are undesired within our circles or homes. Protecting the home from these nasty critters can be as simple as taking off your shoes to avoid tracking in dirt from outside. Most often, these outsiders are found in the stresses of work or other matters outside of a healthy relationship that tend to wander in when we are not looking.

Smudging

Keeping a smudge pot and smudge stick by the front door is always a good idea. Smudge yourself daily as you enter the home. This is akin to old world Catholics' blessing themselves with holy water upon entering their home. On a particularly stressful day, one in which you want your partner to help you through, invite him or her to come out onto the porch and tell your partner all about your day as he or she smudges you. Afterward, return the favor. The idea here is that such matters be left outside the home. Even when the day hasn't been terribly bad, it is still nice for the first person back from work to greet the second at the door for smudging. If you think this is too much for the neighbors' eyes, then step just inside the home.

Mirror Boxes

Mirror boxes are often wood on the outside, but mirrored on the inside. Sometimes they have a small slot on the top for inserting folded pieces of paper. If you can find or build one of these, keep it outside your front door. When you return to an empty home, write on the piece of paper all the outsiders you might have picked up during the day, fold it, insert it into the box, and leave it where it should be: outside!

Once a month, and better it be at the Dark or Waning Moon, meet with your partner by a barbecue grill or fire circle and open the box. Discuss each item that has been written down and inserted into the box over the previous month. If the issue needs to be addressed, do so, and then burn the paper, releasing the outsider into the night air. Afterward is a good time for s'mores, sweets to further banish the outsiders, who are often bitter.

Fertility and Medical Issues

Tarot readers are quick to tell you that the Death card doesn't always mean death. People who belong to fertility religions are quick to tell you that fertility does not always mean birth. What they tend to avoid mentioning is that sometimes the Death card does mean death and sometimes fertility does mean birth. The very nature of our life is found in these two things, birth and death. One begins this particular journey, and the other ends it and starts a new. When considering such important matters as beginnings or endings, we should take care to use the best information available.

Few people enjoy visiting their doctor. However, if Wiccans are true to magick and spellcraft, they should embrace their doctor's visit as if they were visiting Merlin himself. Why? Because there isn't a single thing in medicine and science that wasn't first a part of magick and spellcraft. Before anything is explained, it is first unexplained. Thus, the knowledge your doctor can provide has been built on spells and magicks that have worked so well that somewhere along the way, they became science. Such a transformation does not mean that we should dismiss it, but instead embrace it as the naturally evolved magick. Indeed, in many cultures the word for *magick* and the word for *medicine* are either similar or identical. A friend reports that if you want to find a shop for your spellcraft needs in Jamaica, you should ask for a drugstore.

There are many important medical issues surrounding conception, fertility, and other areas where spellcraft is often consulted. Infertility can often be a sign of very serious medical conditions. With such matters, I strongly suggest that you both consult your family doctor and read *The Fastest Way to Get Pregnant Naturally* by Christopher Williams, M.D., and *Taking Charge of Your Fertility* by Toni Weschler. With the consent of your doctor and practices spelled out in these books, there are additional charms, amulets, and spells you can use to improve your odds. (If you are interested in decreasing your odds, the latter book discusses natural forms of birth control.)

Fertility and Conception Charms

When people think of fertility charms, they tend to think of jewelry and statuary representatives of large-breasted, full-figured fertility Goddesses. Rarely does the image of an erect penis come to mind. In our many attempts to rebirth the ancient fertility religions, we seem to have forgotten the male half of conception. This is unfortunate when we consider the fact that the male role in the acts leading to conception is just as subject to failure (if not more) as the female. Ancient Roman Pagans must have known this, as the image of the erect penis once filled their art and jewelry.

Here we find a great opportunity for discovery. Let the woman fashion a phallic symbol for the man and the man create a Fertility Goddess symbol for the woman. Doing so together with discussion of the future child will greatly enhance the experience and discovery, and you'll have a great time joking about your partner's sculpting abilities—or lack of. Ideally, the charms are made with pottery clay, but most people do not have access to a kiln. If you feel brave, you can purchase clay rated at "cone 04" and then ask a local ceramic shop to fire it for you, but that might be a bit embarrassing. An alternative is either air-dried or oven-baked clay. Do not use the plastic variety, as it is not porous.

Charms don't have to be perfect, but they should be functional. If you plan to wear them around your neck, make sure you include a hole for the cord or chain. Once the charms have been fired, baked, or dried, anoint them with your favorite essential oil from the following list and give them to each other. Each day, anoint your partner's charm with the same oil (do not remove it from around their neck).

➢ Essential oils for the masculine charm include cinnamon, clove, rosemary, and peppermint.

➢ Essential oils for the feminine charm include patchouli, jasmine, lemon, myrrh, and sandalwood.

These oils can also be used on store-purchased charms, but if you plan on using them on anything made of metal or other non-porous material, carry the charms in a small cloth bag and anoint the bag daily.

Fertility and Conception Sachets

Call them sachets, medicine bags, or mojo bags, they amount to the same thing: bundles of herbs and other items that are typically worn around the neck on a cord or carried in the pocket. You can either purchase or sew an actual bag, or you can place the mixture in the center of a piece of cloth and then draw the cloth up and bind it with cord to keep it closed. Fertility sachets are most commonly of the color green, but brown is sometimes used to symbolize the fertility of rich soil.

Following the same guidelines for oils listed with fertility charms, gather or purchase dried herbs. Instead of grinding them with a mortar and pestle, select two or three of each and as a couple, grind them together palm to palm for the preparation of each. Prior to making love, each should remove a bit of their herbal mixture and hold it in the palm, the couple can then place palms together and grind the mixtures even further, mixing each and then scattering the finally ground plant material around their bed just prior to making love. As you do, visualize the essence of your love mingling with your partner through your palms, a bit of each charging the mixture.

Inspiring Lust and Influencing Moods

Patchouli reportedly heightens a woman's desire for her man; vanilla is said to cause a man to desire his woman; and chocolate seems to have the same effect on both men and women. But much better results can be attained by observing your partner's reactions and remembering them. So the answer to what works is really found where the fun is, in experimentation. Candles, food, incense, perfume, and oils can all have tremendous influence, but they will only be effective if you remember which ones solicit the desired response from yourself and your partner. Here, again, is where the couple's Book of Shadows comes in.

Obtain your lover's permission before experimenting randomly with his or her senses. Once that consent has been received, conduct yourself covertly, not letting your partner know what it is that you are testing until you are able to draw conclusions from the experiment.

How lustful was your partner after a massage with almond-scented massage oil? What about patchouli? What happens when you serve vegetarian meals vs. meat? Does your partner respond to essential oils worn on your body? What about perfume? By observing your partner's reactions to controlled stimuli, you can learn his or her triggers. Because this careful observation takes into account the many differences in human beings, it is far more effective than anything you will read in a book. Share your discoveries with your partner and include them in your couple's Book of Shadows.

General Celebrations and the 13 Steps of Wiccan Ritual

So you can see how Wiccan couples can practice their religion as any other religion would. We celebrate both Sabbat and special occasions within the boundaries of our religion, while allowing others to take part in those celebrations without being Wiccan or being scared by any of the spooky formality that so many insist are a part of our family religion. The following steps illustrate a general celebration.

1. **Lustral bath.**

Conducted by the Host and Hostess prior to the event. Hopefully you need not ask your guests to bathe prior to a social event. If you do, maybe you should look for different guests.

2. **Dress.**

Just as the ancient Pagans probably wore the casual clothing of the time for casual events and formal clothing of the time for formal events, we can dress in the appropriate outfits for our modern times.

3. **Preparing the temple.**

Prepare and clean your home prior to guests arriving.

4. **Smudging and asperging.**

Your guests will probably think that smudging at the doorway is fashionable.

5. **Offering the challenge.**

Meet guests at the door and ask them to be your guest.

6. **Casting the circle.**

This was already done during the home blessing. In spooky circles, it is common to ask that no one leave except by the "door," that door being formally cut into the circle by the High Priest or Priestess. In the real world, the doors are those connecting the outside world to the home. It is customary for the Host or Hostess to open this door to allow guests to enter or leave.

7. **Inviting the Quarters.**

It would be appropriate to offer a prayer at supper to thank the four winds for bringing your guests safely to your home, as well as to protect your home as you enjoy the evening.

8. Inviting the Lord and Lady.

The Host holds the chair for female guests; the Hostess holds the chair for male guests. Perhaps a toast by the Host to thank his wife for her role in the meal as well as in his life. In return, a toast by the Hostess to thank her husband for his role in the evening as well as in her life.

9. The symbolic Great Rite.

The symbolic Great Rite could be something as simple as the Host and Hostess kissing prior to taking their seats.

10. Body of the ritual.

The meal and activities afterward, the interaction, and the joy shared by kith and kin all contribute to the body of the ritual.

11. Thanking the Lord and Lady.

The Host thanks Hostess for her efforts towards building a wonderful evening. The Hostess thanks the Host for the same.

12. Thanking the Quarters.

Wish friends well, offer a blessing that the same winds that brought them safely to the celebration return them safely home.

13. Opening the circle.

Hold the door for your guests to leave.

9   Ouc Childcen

*I have a dream that my four little children will
one day live in a nation where they will not be
judged by the color of their skin
but by the content of their character.*

—Martin Luther King, Jr. (1929–1968)

Introduction

A world in which "Love is the Law" might not be realized
in our generation, but if our children see our attempts (successful
or not) they too will strive for that good. Upon becoming a parent,
a child who has been raised to love will love. This is as it should
be, because it is in the very nature of fit parents to desire better
for their children.

Unfortunately, sometimes this noble cause becomes resent-
ment. Many Wiccans resent their parents for having had them
baptized or in other ways dedicated to a religion that was not
their own choosing. They hesitate doing so to their own children
because they do not want to repeat the mistake. They want
better for their children. It is noble to want better for your
children, but I have to tell you that in this quest to be better
parents, some Wiccans have become really nutty.

I have a friend who became one of these nuts for a time. Before her child could so much as speak, our little circle of friends was issued guidelines of interaction with her baby. The first was that the use of the word *child* was out because it might stunt her son's natural growth. Likewise, the term *young adult* might artificially accelerate her son's growth. Of course *little one* might cause her baby to feel inferior. The words *man*, *son*, and *boy* were forbidden because using those words might cast undo gender rolls on her offspring. When she decided the word *offspring* might artificially force the connection between mother and, well, and "it," we ran out of words to use. Fortunately for us, and more importantly her child, she came to her senses, and we no longer have to address her son as "it." Not long after this very welcome change, we welcomed her son at his Wiccaning.

You see, that is exactly what a Wiccaning is. It is a welcoming. Where some might see the rite of Wiccaning as dedicating a child to our religion without his or her consent, I see it more as the consensual dedication of the family and community to its new child. It is the formal act of welcoming a new life into our law, but not so much to say that this child will have to accept that law, rather to say that our law now accepts that child. It is a promise on the part of the parents and the community that they will raise that child with love in such a way as the child will in turn be one who loves. What better way to give our children a better world than to give them the tools in which they can make our world better? Those tools are that same dedicated family and community on which our children can build.

I can't quote her perfectly on this one, but I distinctly recall hearing Starhawk talk in front of a university on the issue of Witchcraft. In her presentation, she commented that she had never given birth. But from talking to friends who had, she could imagine no experience more profound. She added that if men gave birth, all of the historic cathedrals that were built by men would be decorated with images of the crowning of a child's head and other images of birth. (Ah, there is the Starhawk that I have come to know and love, untouched by the insanity that I described in *Wicca Spellcraft for Men*.)

Like Starhawk, I have never given birth, which is a very good thing because I am male. I, too, have friends who have described childbirth as a religious experience. I, too, believe that if the folks in charge of building those cathedrals had been the folks who bear children, the event would be celebrated in many vivid expressions incorporated into their very structure. But history is history and that has not been the case. While we can strive to improve our world, we must also recognize it for what it is.

Birth: Who Will Deliver the Child?

In the extreme examples of history (usually slavery), we can find examples of women, who, while tending crops gave birth, and then immediately returned to work. In less extreme examples of history, we see women giving birth at home with little assistance. There we see incredibly low survival rates.

That same nutty friend from the introduction to this chapter had an opinion on this issue. She wanted her birth attended only by the women of her coven. Better our children be delivered by those who are already trained. In this case, this usually means doctors, but in some cases I understand there are other professionals (midwives) with equal training.[1] Who is more sacred than the person who will give our children and our mothers the best chance of survival?

Birth: Location

As if not having a doctor present wasn't bad enough, my nutty friend described a deep elder forest as the ideal location. Indeed, some studies have suggested that home births might be a healthier way to go if one has a healthy child. But what happens when, to our surprise, the child is not healthy? That deep elder forest doesn't usually come equipped with a telephone for dialing 911. Even at home, the response time of such a phone call is far slower than the almost immediate assistance that we find in hospitals.

For the most part, neither cathedral nor delivery room has been built by those who give birth. This is why religious structures have not shown a connection to the religious nature of childbirth. But this is also why the structures of childbirth have not shown a connection to the religious nature of childbirth.

This does not mean we should give up on the practice of building structures of religion. While most Wiccan groups are not financially capable of erecting new cathedrals and temples as places of worship, we do what we can with what we have. We let our hearts guide us and erect temples in basements, backyards, and spare bedrooms, because those places suit both need and heart.

In choosing the place where our children will be born, we should do the same: We should find a place that suits both need and heart. Here we see the medical need of having properly trained people (and the emergency equipment that we hope we won't need). But here, too, we see the heart's desire not to bring our children first into the overly sterile world of a delivery room that might threaten their emotional development. Fortunately, we no longer have to gamble on our children's physical health to ensure their emotional health. Hospitals have heard our voices and they have begun providing heartwarming birthing rooms in addition to the standard heart-chilling delivery room.

A lot of us have tremendous fears about people trained in the area of medicine (see the acknowledgments for mine). But when it comes to the trend among Wiccans to home-birth without the assistance of medical staff, we are again living in the Dark Ages. After all, it was the Church who once forbade doctors from helping women deliver children, because their scripture insisted that the pain of childbirth was punishment for original sin. Instead of rejecting the blessings of modern medicine in the birth of our children, better we do what our religion does best: embrace both old and new. In a religion that celebrates birth, what place could be more sacred than a room that was built specifically for that purpose?

Birth: Delivery

You are probably getting tired of hearing about that nutty friend of mine, but I have one more story. She insisted that her delivery take place with absolutely no drugs, no episiotomy, and, of course, no C-section. In this respect, she got exactly what she wished for. She was a good little Dianic Feminist Witch right up to the point when she screamed for drugs to subdue the nearly unbearable pain. Unfortunately, it was too late. As I recall, it took more than a husband stitch[2] to put her back together. But even if the husband stitch had repaired the tearing, it would not have mended her broken pelvis. Instead, she spent the first few weeks with her child in absolute agony. Now is that the Wiccan way?

> "To the woman He said, 'I will greatly multiply
> Your pain in childbirth,
> In pain you will bring forth children;
> Yet your desire will be for your husband,
> And he will rule over you.'"
>
> —(Genesis 3:16).
> From the *New American Standard Bible*

The very idea that anyone (including the Creator by any name) should "greatly multiply" a woman's "pain in childbirth" is obscene. I hope this seems as ridiculous to Christians as some of Gardner's rantings do to Wiccans.

Then what of natural childbirth? Again, it is only by our Law that we have survived. In this case, it is love that has caused the medical community to rise in the hopes of easing suffering and pain. Remember, doctors are all sworn to the Oath of Hippocrates, better known as the Hippocratic Oath (see Appendix F), which begins:

> "I swear by Apollo the physician, and Æsculapius, and Hygeia, and Panacea, and al! the gods and goddesses, that according to my ability and judgment, I will keep this oath and its stipulations..."

In its ancient form, this oath demands that doctors "...follow that system of regimen which, according to my ability and judgment, I consider for the benefit of my patients, and abstain from whatever is deleterious and mischievous."

So then, when a doctor acts of oath and heart, if that doctor recommends pain relief, C-section, delivery room birth, or anything else that seems not to be natural, we see in our law and the Oath of Hippocrates that those things are themselves not only natural, but most definitely as rooted in Pagan ways as the oath itself.

Other Helpful Bits From Friends

➢ **Amulets, Jewelry, and Sacred Symbols:** Although most doctors won't tell you this, they are usually more than willing to let you wear sacred symbols during childbirth. If you arrange it ahead of time, they will most often be willing to cover the jewelry with a sterile bandage and surgical tape.

➢ **Chanting:** Okay, so they might not let you burn candles, smolder incense, or dance naked around a bonfire, but I am sure most doctors would prefer to hear focused chanting rather than scattered screaming. In fact, many natural childbirth methods now incorporate chants to focus the mind off pain. Why not incorporate your own words into these chants? I suggest using the names of the many archetypes that protect women during this time.

➤ **Coaches:** If a woman has not the father of her child or other beloved partner for the delivery, I am told there is no better coach than her own mother.

➤ **Waiting Room Circles:** It might seem like the whole family should be present for birth, but doctors tend to think they get in the way and usually only allow the father or coach to be present in the delivery room. This makes the waiting room the ideal place for circles to raise blessings for both mother and child. Although you might think the waiting room is a very busy place, I have found most to be rather lonely. But even when there is a group of people you do not know, you will be amazed to find how little one's specific religion seems to matter in the waiting room of a maternity ward. There, everyone is often willing to hold hands and pray with others to whatever Gods and Goddesses they may. Ah, there may be hope for us yet.

➤ **Ice Chips and Raspberry Leaves:** If your doctor tells you that the only refreshment a mother should having during childbirth is ice chips, why not ask the doctor if you can bring your own ice chips? Make them out of raspberry-leaf tea or any of the other herbs that your doctor says can't hurt and lore tells us will help.

➤ **Birthing Rooms**: Most hospitals now offer birthing rooms. They might cost a little more than birth in a standard delivery room, but they are a whole lot more relaxing than that standard delivery room and a whole lot less expensive than moving an entire medical staff with equipment for every possible problem to your own home. Instead, we can move those items that make us comfortable to the birthing room.

The Rite of Wiccaning

The Wiccan rite of Wiccaning is not akin to the Christian rite of Baptism in at least two very important ways:

1. Wiccaning: Dedication of the religion to child.
   Baptism: Dedication of the child to religion.

2. Wiccaning: Pointing out that the child is born within Law (love).
   Baptism: Pointing out that the child is born outside of Law (original sin).

As do all Wiccan rites, the Wiccaning follows the basic 13 steps and is very similar to the rite of handfasting, not only in appearance, but in symbolism. Where the handfasting marks the promises of two people to each other, the Wiccaning marks the promises of a family and community to the child.

Lustral Bath

Without the limitations of most bathtubs, the lustral bath might be shared by mother, father, and child in much the way bathing is shared by family members in many other cultures. I say might, because we do not live in those cultures. If you are, as I am, culturally challenged in this issue, then let both mother and father bathe their child, but then let one retire to their own lustral bath while the other tends the child, and visa versa.

Dress

For a time, my mother was very fond of showing off my baby bathtub pictures. She knew it tormented me and seemed to want to do so every time I introduced her to a date. Although it might seem that having your child skyclad for the Wiccaning would desensitize your child to such an issue, I would rather not encourage such photo opportunities. I was naked in that bathtub and still am not desensitized to the picture. Besides, the way the courts are going, you might be arrested for child pornography should one of your guests snap a picture. In my estimation, it is better your child be dressed as his or her age dictates and best the parents be dressed in accordance with modern customs of rites of passage.

Preparing the Temple

Here, attention to the child's needs far supersede the needs of your guests. Sufficient warmth and subdued lighting should be at the top of your list of concerns.

Smudging and Asperging

Best to go light on the smoke and to smudge guests as they arrive rather than when standing in circle. Then assemble the guests in a circle, but facing outward rather than in.

Offering the Challenge and the Outsiders

From outside the circle, the mother and father address their guests:

Mother: "We have gathered you here to meet our new child"

Father: "We have gathered you here to give our child the protection of Law"

Mother: "We have gathered you here to bless our child with that Law"

Father: "For that law is Love"

Mother: "Let anyone who would not meet, protect, and bless our child leave now"

Father: "And with them take all forces whom might seek this child harm."

Casting the Circle

With child in arms, father goes to just outside the eastern-most part of the circle and holds his child to the first man he sees and says, for example,

"This is my son Christopher. Will you promise to welcome, protect, and bless him as if you were his father?"

Guests should answer in their own words. Should any man decline, he should be politely asked to leave the circle and become a spectator. The father moves clockwise and addresses every man in circle in kind.

With child in arms, mother goes to just outside the easternmost part of the circle and holds her child to the first woman she sees.

"This is my son Christopher. Will you promise to welcome, protect, and bless him as if you were his mother?"

Guests should answer in their own words. Should any woman decline, she should be politely asked to leave the circle and become a spectator. The mother moves clockwise and addresses every woman in circle in kind.

Mother (still holding child):
"Please continue to face outward as our child first enters this circle of family and friends."

The mother, father, and child go to the center of the circle, where the father speaks:

Father: "Before you is the world without friend or family, now please turn and see our child in the whole of your family and friendship for the first time."

Mother: "Call it church, temple, circle, or the house of the Divine, it is most certainly cast before you in love."

Inviting the Quarters

Here, it is best if the father's father stands at the East Quarter (Air), the father's mother stands at the North Quarter (Earth), the mother's mother stands at the West Quarter (Water) and the mother's father stand at the South Quarter (Fire). However, the interaction between grandparents is also nice, so you might want to switch these roles such that they are as in the handfasting rite. Failing the presence or willingness of the grandparents, close friends can stand for them.

Here we see one of the almost hidden mysteries of our religion. We count the number three as sacred (hence the triskele), in that it represents to the Holy Trinity as:

> Mother, Father, and Child
>
> Maiden, Mother, and Crone
>
> Master, Father, and Sage
>
> Above, Below, and Center

This Holy Trinity is only the beginning of the story. In the middle of this story, we count the number five as sacred (hence the pentagram) as Earth, Air, Fire, and Water crowned with spirit. But in ritual, we find that spirit in our own hearts (center circle). So when we combine the sacred three with the sacred five, those things that are said to be child, center, and spirit are as one. Hence the end and the whole of the story is represented no more strongly than in this rite. For here we see the number seven as even more sacred than either three or five. Here we see the seven directions of our circle. What I see as a much better symbol for Wicca than either borrowing the triskele from the Celts or the pentagram from the Christians:[3] the seven-pointed star that represents this cycle of life and the circle which represents the family and friends that supports it.

East:	Father's Father
North:	Father's Mother
West:	Mother's Mother
South:	Mother's Father
Above:	Father
Below:	Mother
Center:	Child

The Quarters are then invited in the normal way, by bringing tools to the center altar and uniting them. But when East and North are united, the mother asks of the father's parents:

"This is my son, Christopher. Will you promise to welcome, protect, and bless him as if he were the man who fathered him?"

When West and South are united, the father asks of the mother's parents:

"This is my son, Christopher. Will you promise to welcome, protect, and bless him as if he were the woman who mothered him?"

Invitation to Our Lord and Lady

Mother (holding child) invites Lord:

"As lover, you came to my bed. Will you come to my child as father to welcome, protect, and bless him as your son?"

Father should answer in his own words. If he accepts, mother gives him their child.

Father (holding child) invites Lady:

"As lover, you, too, came to my bed. Will you come to my child as mother to welcome, protect, and bless him as your son?"

Mother should answer in her own words.

The Great Rite

If the mother accepts, both hold the child, and the couple kisses, as the symbolic Great Rite. They then open their couple's Book of Shadows to a page that should read similarly:

"On this day, _____(date)_____, I promise that I will welcome, protect, and bless Christopher as my son"

Below that statement, mother signs on the left and father signs on the right.

Body of the Ritual
The body of this ritual is receiving gifts for the child.

Thanking the Lord and Lady
The mother and father thank each other for their role in the life of their child.

Thanking the Quarters
The parents thank the grandparents for their role in the life of their children. It is also a time when the grandparents' promise should be signed with not only name, but mailing address, phone number, and any additional contact information as might be necessary in the future, should that promise be called upon.

Walking Down and Opening the Circle
In large circles, this might not be practical. But if the circle is small, you can walk it down by bringing the couple's Book of Shadows to the eastern-most part of the circle. Then, moving counterclockwise, ask each person in attendance to sign as the grandparents did. From a legal viewpoint, I suggest the signatures of at least the grandparents be in the order in which those two couples will fulfill their promise, should something happen to the child's parents.

10 Handpartings: The Bonds That Break

*If you love something,
set it free.
If it comes back,
it was and always will be yours.
If it never returns,
it was never yours to begin with.*

—Author Unknown

Introduction

If it is strange that there are very few books on the rite of handfasting, it must be absolutely bizarre that there are virtually none on the subject of handpartings. With the divorce rate at more than 50 percent, one must ask the question: Does it reflect the failure of the institution of marriage itself, or could it be a sign of something a bit more pleasant? In my 36 years, I have held distinctly different opinions on the subject. In my youth (before wed), I thought marriage was forever. I met this beautiful and spirited woman in Germany, and it just seemed natural that she and I become wife and husband. The marriage had its ups and downs, but more or less, it was level. Without going into details, poor communications led to the union's undoing, and I was devastated. During our relationship we had occasionally fought, but at no time prior to its undoing was the word *divorce* ever spoken by either. In my misery, I developed a deep hate for the woman I once loved.

Now, years after the event, we have come to know each other as friends. I have come to the conclusion that we must have been ill-fated and should count our divorce as the blessing that we both might again find love rather than hinder that discovery with involvement in a failing marriage.

Of course, during the years that followed, I did do more or less the same thing with other relationships of the heart, perhaps missing Ms. Right because I spent so much time with Ms. Wrong. But eventually, I learned that we all have an addiction to real love. It is the one thing that is important. But if we feed that addiction with its generic equivalent, we often become blind to the fact that we are doing without the very thing that we need. You see, real love is a healing force, but its generic equivalent is little more than a pain reliever. It might feel really good, but it does nothing to address the healing of the heart. Wouldn't it be nice if we had rituals that did?

In my view of Wicca, the rite of handparting should never be performed during the Winter months. These short months are better served as a time of reflection rather than action, as they are when our emotions often ride at the lowest. Our hearts are at their weakest at this time of the year and the rite of handparting should never be called to strike an enemy at its weakest. Rather, it should lift one's partner and oneself from a union that is not mutually beneficial. The exception to this is when life offers no choice for timing, which is most often the case with the first rite of handparting.

In my view of handparting, there are three separate instances:

1. The first rite of hand parting and the third *handfasting* (a death promise). This preserves the cycle of union, separation, and reunion.

2. The rite of handparting in which both parties agree it is best that they part so each might find love again.

3. The rite of handparting to which one party does not agree.

I have given these rites order for the purpose of discussion. This is not to say that one handparting should be performed after the other, or that they should all be performed as the whole of the process. Each rite is whole, in as much as anything can be, and is used as circumstances dictate.

The First Rite of Handparting (Also the Third Rite of Handfasting)

The first rite of handparting is associated with the Crone and Sage stage of life. This is the promise that although fate might separate partners in this lifetime, the partners are each free to return to the other's side if they will. It is a reminder that love cannot be forced, but also that with love all force must surrender, including death.

As such, this rite is not reserved for only partners who have been united in the type of union shared by lovers. Just as death does not discriminate, this rite is for all who would part from love in its many forms. Husband and wife, child and parent, or any manifestation of kith and kin.

In some aspects, the first rite of handparting is also the third rite of handfasting. This is the death-bed promise. This rite should not be performed earlier than a year and a day after a rite of handfasting, nor when love remains, because it most certainly is not an act of breaking vows. However, here an exception is made for the extremely old and those who might find death prior to the end of the time of commitment by handfasting.

Life does not always give us the opportunity for ritual. When I heard of my father's pending death, it was via the Red Cross. At the time, I was a soldier serving his country abroad. My Commanding Officer asked me what I wanted to do. It wasn't really a decision in my mind, rather a course of action. My father was dying, so I was going home.

By the time I returned to the States, my father (bless his stubborn ass) had insisted on returning home to die. My mother (bless her warm heart) granted his wish, and drove him to their home to watch him die. Fate would have it that I would be the one to watch, but not before his body became little more than a withered image of the man inside.

Now my father wasn't Pagan in namesake. Although baptized Lutheran, he was more of an agnostic philosopher. But he did live by our law and encouraged me to find that law where I willed. He couldn't burn incense, chant, or do any of the standard functions typically associated with Wiccan ritual, or so much as stand. The room in which he rested wasn't large enough to cast a circle, and I was sure incense would have been a bad idea. To be honest, I didn't even think about a rite of handparting. Instead, I just sat next to him each night wondering how and why he clung to life when he was so obviously in great pain. Then the night that brought my understanding, he stopped breathing.

I waited, terrified that my waiting was the wrong thing to do, but not wanting to bring further grief to my mother should this not be the moment of his death. When I could stand it no more, I woke her in tears. Having prepared for his death for months, she calmly walked down the stairs to her husband's death bed. To my surprise, he was very much alive. It seems that even in health, he had sleep apnea. My mother returned to her bed and I returned to my tears, but not for my father's pending death. No, my tears were for his life and for the many times in that life that I had not told him how much I loved him.

Since I had returned, whenever I looked at my father I saw that he was no longer whole. When he looked at me, I could tell he was looking through morphine-filtered eyes. But in my tears and in that moment, I saw him whole again and I could tell that he saw me through eyes that were no longer clouded. Maybe men have natural barriers against each other, but it was the first moment we had ever shared completely defenseless of the other, me in my tears and he in his illness. He took my hand and although it was instantly clear that absolutely nothing need be said, we spent the rest of that night trying to make sense of our lives. His last words to me were, "You should go to sleep, Andrew." He passed the next morning.

My mother found her husband dead in that hospital bed the next morning. By his side, I slept in his favorite chair. She tried to wake me, but I asked that she let us sleep. I am not sure if she understood, but in my dream, my father was still very much alive, and in that dream, unlike life, we remained completely defenseless of each other. Playing pool and talking without any sense of competition.

I doubt very much I could have had that dream time if I had been more focused on the ritual of handparting rather than the real life handparting that we shared holding hands and trying to make sense of our lives. I miss him so.

Unfortunately, moments like that are few. I say unfortunately, because in their great rarity, they can't touch the hearts of all they should. I told you that the experience of once wanting to take my own life led me to become an author. That in the very moment I faced death, I found life and love (Goddess), and as a result I turned back death (my illness) with that love. Although, in my father's confrontation, his physical death was not turned back by love, the death of our relationship was. You see, things weren't always the best between my father and his sons. Oh, he tried and he did know love, but boys and their fathers do not always see eye to eye. I am not sure how I would have felt about him should we not have had that evening holding hands, but I do know how my brother feels about him— he did not have that night.

Part of my drive in writing for the Wiccan community is found in my desire to share the love that I found in my confrontation with death. Here, that drive is for my brother and for the many people who might face the death of a loved one without an opportunity for those last words. It is said that funerals are more for the living than for the dead. Then why is it the dead can hear our words but we cannot hear theirs?

So wherever this rite calls on Host and Hostess, I use those words only for ease of writing. The two leading this rite should be the one who is closest to death and the one who is dearest to that person's heart. This will most likely be husband or wife, but not always. It is important that this rite be for both wed and unwed, because no one should feel as if they will die alone.

The Ritual

Lustral Bath

The peel of lemons and oranges may serve well to heighten the lustral bath prior to this rite as they lend themselves well to friendships and the types of unions addressed by this rite. Passion flower also promotes these unions, however it will also give a red/purple tint to the water. Some might be overwhelmed by the connection between this color and blood.

Dress

The focus of dress in this rite is to dress for oneself rather than for guests. Dress as you would in life that you are remembered in life.

Preparing the Temple

The temple should be a grand hall if you wish to share with a grand number of guests, but better it be your own home or backyard if it is with a small group of close friends.

Smudging and Asperging

Sage will do, but better it be pure gum Arabic smoldered liberally over coals. For asperges, use holy water (best made as described on page 107).

Offering the Challenge

The challenge should be issued much the way I described at either the first or second handfasting, however, everyone should be facing outward as in the Wiccaning. Each guest should hold a folded piece of paper on which any grievances with either Host or Hostess should be written. Visible without unfolding should be the guest's name. If a guest has no grievance, they should hold a blank piece of paper, folded just in the same manner, and also bearing his or her name on the outside.

This rite is as a death promise, so there will likely be one member of the couple who is gravely ill. In that case, the one who has taken ill sits in the center of the circle. If instead, neither is facing death, but both are of sufficient age as to warrant the rite, then the elder of the two sits at the center of the circle and the other issues the challenge:

> "We have come here to celebrate both union and parting. For it is said that we are separated for the sake of union. We are here to insure that as merrily as we met, so merrily do we part. Here we will cast our circle and here it will not be broken but when all grievances are settled. I will come to you to collect any grievance; if you would stay, then offer me the grievance. If you would not, then take that grievance with you and become not a member of this circle of kith and kin by your own choice."

Casting the Circle

When all is ready, the person who is eldest or who might shortly die rings a bell, opens the couple's Book of Shadows, and lights a candle to announce the beginning of the rite. The healthier or younger of the couple goes to just outside the eastern-most portion of the circle. There, he or she moves clockwise, retrieving all grievances into a basket. Each person is warned:

"Leave this circle of family and friends if you are not willing to stay until each grievance is resolved. But better you stay within this circle of family and friends."

Once this person has gone full circle:

"My [Lord or Lady] would now cast this circle, but I in [his or her] stead, for in union we swore to each other's role."

The idea here is that the healthier or younger person casts the circle once for his or her role, and also once for the partner's role.

When finished this person goes to the side of his or her partner in the center of the circle, and says:

"Before you is the world without Family. Please turn and face center. Although I have cast this circle with athame, here you see the real circle created by your attendance. Here we see the real walls of a church, temple, and circle built with kith and kin rather than stick and stone."

Inviting the Quarters

Ideally, the quarters would be invited by the Host and Hostess' son and his wife, as well as daughter and her husband. Alternatively, by the Host and Hostess's two sons and two daughters. But life doesn't always give us ideal circumstances. So, if children are not available or willing, let two mated Quarters be invited by two who are themselves mates and dear to the Hostess. Let the other two Quarters be invited by a couple that is dear to the Host.

Inviting the Lord and Lady

This should be in the order and nature of this rite, but in the words of the heart.

> One speaks: "In life we were [husband and wife, son and father, or whatever fits]. Will you be the same in death and beyond?"
>
> The other speaks the same.

From the couple's Book of Shadows, each member of the couple should read and sign their last vows to the other in so much as saying any grievance of this lifetime shall not follow us into the next. That as in life, both are free to stay if they will, but go if they must. The idea is that if love should unite them again in the next life, they not be hindered by grievances from this life.

The Great Rite

Here the couple is challenged to create symbolism appropriate to the couple. In the case of husband and wife, this might be the standard lowering of an athame into a chalice of wine. But in cases of father and son, this might be the act of breaking a sword over knee (best it be a wooden sword) and then father throwing one half clear of the circle in one direction and son tossing the other in the other direction, symbolically destroying male barriers and scattering them. In the case of mother and daughter, it might be the act of pouring two chalices into one and then each drinking of the common chalice.

To those who would say the Great Rite is symbolic sex only, I say hogwash. Even the actual act of sex is not the Great Rite itself. The Great Rite is the union of two souls.

Body of the Ritual

In other rites, the outsiders are asked to leave. In this rite, the aim is to not simply remove them from our circle but to destroy them such that they do not hinder us on our path to the summerland or on our return. In this rite, the outsiders are represented in those grievances. The one who collected the grievances pulls the first and calls the name on the paper but does not unfold the paper. The one named comes to the center of the circle.

Either Host or Hostess speaks for both and offers a gift that should serve as a focus for memories of the one who is parting more than anything of great value (birthstones come to mind). The gift need not be the same for each person as this might be a beautiful time to pass on a family heirloom (maybe a wedding gown or favorite book):

"This may be the last thing I can give you."

The gift is given.

Of course this idea is not new. But I credit it to my father, who shared it with me in Germany. In so doing, he let me know that his cancer had returned. After a short visit, I had to board a train and return to my unit, and my family was moving on to Italy. My father took me aside and handed me a stack of German bills, telling me that he and my mother wouldn't have time to change it for Italian currency. I glanced at the bills long enough to know it wasn't pocket change. I figured the exchange rate had slipped his mind and he didn't realize what he was handing me, so I protested. "This may be the last thing I can give you." I boarded the train and prayed in tears that he was wrong.

My father *was* wrong. He still had one thing to give me and it would be given the night before his death. He gave me his time and listened as we held hands and let go of any grievance I had, so that I would forever remember him as a man with whom I have no grievances.

The one whose name was called is then handed the piece of paper. In accordance with that person's will, he or she can either cast the paper into a smoldering cauldron (any safe fire source will do) or read it, hold hands, and cry (if it should happen). But there and then all things must be settled, less one not be true to our law and face the inherent penalties of that lie.

Either without grievance or having grievance that has been settled, each guest signs the couple's Book of Shadows below the couple's signatures, where it shall state in the couples choice of words:

"I have no grievance that should hold until we meet again."

Thanking the Lord and Lady

Prior to the rite, the Host and Hostess should have written their final thanks to their partner for being a loving spouse. The thanking of the Lord and Lady takes the form of reading those pages and signing them.

Thanking the Quarters

Prior to this rite, those who stood in the Quarters should have written a page for the Book of Shadows that thanks the couple for their union and for (in the case of their children) their very lives. The thanking of the Quarters takes the form of reading those pages, signing them, and including them in the couple's Book of Shadows. Because any couple that would part in this way is a fine example of what a Wiccan should be, their Book of Shadows becomes *our* lore, to be shared later by the family, if they will.

Walking Down and Opening the Circle

If possible, the couple should walk down the circle together and say good-bye to each member as they do. Once the circle has been walked down, the couple should return to center where one should ring the bell, close the book (tying it shut with the cord from their handfasting if available), extinguish the candle, and as their last public act as a couple (representative of our divine Lord and Lady), they should pass the book to their children or other worthy recipient.

Husband: "Merry did we meet."

Wife: "Merry do we part."

Guests: "And Merry will we meet again."

The Second Rite of Handparting (Both in Agreement)

The second rite of handparting is associated with the Mother and Father stage of life. This is probably the most important handparting because it is often the case that in their union, the couple has indeed become mother and father. Certainly they have created a base of friends that should be assured that, although the couple has parted, friendships remain. This rite is not only the parting of their hearts as lovers, but the assurance that they will not part in their responsibilities to their child, their responsibilities to each other in that capacity, or in the many friendships that they made as a couple.

The second rite of handparting can be likened to a dissolution of marriage, in that it is performed with both partners in agreement. But this is not a bitter act. Instead, it is the happy release of two people who found the bonds of their handfasting too restrictive. Perhaps they grew apart or maybe they were just never meant to be. Either way, better they part friends and not hinder each other's quest for new love.

This rite should only take place if three important qualifiers exist. First, both must agree and welcome it. Second, the promise of a year and a day or for as long as love shall stay has been met. Third and lastly, if the union was made legal in any way, the commitments of the law of the land be addressed prior to the law of the heart. I say this because it is next to impossible to move on if you are returned again and again to this ending point, even if that return is by the courts. Better you be done with all matters of the union before you end the union.

The second rite of handfasting can be conducted as the first, however, the parting vows should not be in the order of one who would part from death. Instead, they should be written and read in the way two would part one relationship while not begrudging the formation of another. The other difference is that the couple's Book of Shadows should not be passed to the next generation in praise. Instead, it should be given to them to keep should the couple ever reunite. If that should not be the case, because we have plenty of examples of failure, the book should be destroyed upon the death of either member.

The Third Rite of Handparting (Only One in Agreement)

The third rite of handparting is associated with the Maiden and Master stage of life. Unfortunately, this is probably the most common because it reflects the current state of handfasting. Earlier, I pointed out that most folks receive the rite of hand-fasting more of whim than of will. So, too, is the case of the handparting among those unions. In those cases, it is usually this handparting that is performed, because only one member of the failed union will stand. The other, acting as a child, won't even bother to give release. Hence, this rite's association with the Maiden and Master, who are often impetuous, even when one of the two has grown.

The third rite of handparting can be likened to the act of divorce. For, as bickering children tend, these two have not been able to resolve their differences, so they have turned to the courts for resolve. Like the second rite, this should not be performed unless the promise of a year and a day has been filled and all matters of the law of the land have been closed. Then, and only then, should you consider this rite without the assistance of your former partner.

Here, too, the rite is much the same, except that when grievances are collected, they are done separately. The partner who is present collects any grievance and addresses it as the rite describes, but the grievances for the missing partner are collected by a stand-in. Those grievances are not heard. Instead, they are placed in the couple's Book of Shadows.

After the rite has concluded, the couple's Book of Shadows should be signed as if both parties agreed and were present, but then sent to the missing party with the signatures of all who stood for the rite and gave consent. If the missing person realizes he should have been there, that person must address each grievance individually and then sign the Book of Shadows, which is then as if it were given as in the second rite.

The Rest of the Family: Those Who Have Not Embraced Our Law

11

We don't bow down to the deities; we work with them to create a better world. This is what makes Wicca a truly participatory religion.

—From *Wicca: A Guide for the Solitary Practitioner* by Scott Cunningham (1956–1993) Llewellyn Worldwide, 1988

Introduction

If our world were perfect, Scott Cunningham would not have pointed out that part of being Wiccan is working to build a better world. We could become wed and then never deal with our in-laws, but what type of a family would that be? We could go along our merry way without ever thinking about the tremendous crimes against humanity that occur every day. But what type of a world would that be?

Our families are not perfect. Our world is not perfect. But having received the law, we have also received not only an invitation to change both family and world, we have received divine instruction to do so. This is because it is impossible to truly know love without wanting others to know it as well.

Some might argue that this is proselytizing and add that many of our leaders have been clear that Wiccans do not proselytize. That is true, although it might be fun. It is not the Wiccan way to stand on a street corner and save souls for our Lord and Lady. But this does not mean we cannot lead by example, and it most certainly does not mean that we should not fight for what is right, rather than sit back and watch either global or local families rip at each other's throats.

Wiccans sometimes seem fond of sitting in the illusion of a moral high ground, as they claim their actions have harmed none. But what of their inaction? It does seem that those quickest to point out their lack of harm are also the slowest into action in the prevention of harm.

It is important to know that even those who have not discovered our law are themselves part of our extended family in much more than a figurative way. Theory currently has it that all of current humanity is descended from one woman, and that with time and genetic divergence (mutation), we simply drifted apart.

These distant relatives might be estranged from us in either their fear of us or our fear of them, but they are just as much family as any other living thing. So let's call them "The Rest of the Family," but in so doing, remember that the "us/them" stance doesn't always work too well because, inevitably, there are more of them than us.

The time in which we live may one day be called the start of World War III. If we escape that potential future, this era will probably be compared to the Neolithic Revolution of some 8,500 years ago.[1] Just as the Neolithic Revolution was a turning point that separated one age of humanity from another, so our current turning point will separate the pending age of humanity from the one in which we live.

The first age of humanity (Maiden and Master) began with the birth of humanity in Africa and continued as we migrated to just about every portion of the Earth. In this Maiden and Master age, we sometimes say we were hunter-gatherers, but, truth be known, we were more of a beach-bum society than hunters and gathers. There is evidence that we did indeed hunt, but there is more evidence that we mostly migrated along coastal areas and fed off of clams, muscles, fish, and other ocean food. When an area became overpopulated or when the pickings became slim, we just moved up the coast.

The second age of humanity (Mother and Father) began with the Neolithic Revolution. This event marked the point when humanity changed its focus from hunting, gathering and beach-bumming to raising livestock, cultivating the land, and becoming city folk. It was when we first started building civilizations of any notable size. This point in history is also when we start to see wars of any notable size. Before the Neolithic Revolution, when two groups came into conflict, the loser could simply move on. But once crops were planted and cities were built, avoiding conflict was not nearly as easy, because there just wasn't an avenue of retreat, and leaving cities often assured death just as much, if not more, than did war.

The third age of humanity (Crone and Sage) is similar to the second in arguments of territory creating tremendous strife. This is the age when we seem to be approaching in a "damn the torpedoes, full speed ahead" method. But today, the disputes faced are more in the territory of thought rather than land. As you are probably aware, the Crone and Sage are often given the same associations as the tarot card of Death. Most often these associations are of new beginnings. But for new beginnings, there is what many tarot readers hesitate to mention: death.

The students in Tiananmen Square were not machine-gunned over land. They were machine-gunned over thought.

So much is this the case that the Chinese government once announced that the students were "infected." Those infections the Chinese government referred to were ideas (specifically, Western ideas). In much the same way as the Chinese government used machine guns to attack Western ideas on June 4, 1989, the terrorists who orchestrated the atrocities of September 11, 2001 did so as an attack on Western ideas.

Today, the flow of information and new ideas is so constant that it is next to impossible to shield oneself from its onslaught. Even terrorists who claim the Western world is the Great Satan use one of the Western world's greatest avenues of communication: the Internet. Where will it end? Well, the advancements in information technologies continue to rush forward, and one can argue that humanity is most vicious when backed up against a wall. So what do we do?

"Think Global, Act Local"
> —A popular bumper sticker
> sold in many Pagan shops

Well, we don't back people up against a wall. Neither you nor I will be able to change the world by attacking the problems head on. We can't solve them overnight and there is a distinct possibility that anything we do today will be too little, too late. However, if we do not first put forth effort, and then hope and pray that our efforts are successful, then we won't have so much as that hope and prayer to hold onto.

I am reminded of an ancient Buddhist story of a master who discovers the secrets of the oceans while meditating on a single drop of rain. In that story, we find the ability to bring into manifestation the changing of our world, not in an attempt to change all of the oceans, but by changing that single drop of rain. If Buddhist teachings are too old for this modern world, then there is that bumper sticker I mentioned.

The Rest of the Family

Think of the rest of the family as everyone who has not yet embraced our law in its many formats. Think of them as the parents who refused to stand at a Quarter in your handfasting, the Catholic who shook hands in church but didn't lift a finger to help his neighbor, and the people who go instantly to rage without ever seeking resolve or mediation.

Don't think so narrowly as only on the letter of our law, but instead on the spirit of that law. Of the Arab-Jewish conflict, Golda Meir (1898–1978) said it would continue "until they love their children more than they hate us." In a time when our children are being fitted with suicide bombs, she couldn't be more correct in her expression of our law. I say "our children" because until we realize that humanity is one family, we will continue to watch "our children" die on the evening news. It will become so commonplace that when we watch it, we won't so much as shed a tear, much less scream in anger. If you haven't lost that heart, then jump from your chair and scream "Stop!" (Did you jump and scream? Come on, it might not help the world, but it will make you feel much better to know that your heart is still alive.)

We need to stop killing each other, stop killing our children, stop killing the world's children, and for the love of whatever god each of us prays to, we must stop this insane path towards the death of not only the human race, but of the planet itself.

Maybe we can affect that single drop of rain. Maybe we can change the message that the Western world is sending. Maybe we can live in accordance with our law, such that others will see and one day embrace that law. That single drop of rain is the personal relationships that we form, and the ocean is changed by how those many single drops of rain interact with the rest of the ocean, the rest of the family.

What Do You Get When You Mix Starhawk With Rush Limbaugh?

It sounds like the beginning of a tremendously funny joke doesn't it? I have no idea what the punch line is, but this sort of combination is exactly what many of us will face when we fall in love. Better we address the issue now, rather than become the butt of the joke later.

Love doesn't know boundaries of race or creed. It certainly doesn't dabble in politics. It knows only matters of the heart. When two people are united as a couple, their families are also united. Sometimes this can seem like the blending of oil and water. But what most people do not know is that water and oil can be blended. In fact, this is one of the processes necessary to make soap (just ask a former dominatrix). All you have to do is find the correct emulsifier. Once that magickal ingredient is found, one might be able to unite such seemingly polar opposites as Starhawk and Rush Limbaugh. Without that emulsifier, we can't have soap and without soap, people just stink up the place.

I have never met either Starhawk or Rush Limbaugh in person. I don't know if they have ever met each other. Although it might well kill the event I hold every year, I would love to invite each to the Real Witches Ball. Unfortunately, their speaking fees are well beyond my grasp, and I doubt either would think the event was prestigious enough to warrant their attendance. As I am sure you can imagine, putting these two together would probably provide great entertainment, especially if you are a fan of World Wrestling Entertainment (WWE). But it is not for entertainment value that I bring up these two celebrities.

We live in an age of information revolution. Because the Western world leads this revolution in its development of technology for disseminating information, it is not surprising that it is Western ideas are at the front of this revolution. This is where we find both Starhawk and Rush Limbaugh. Two internationally known celebrities who seem to offer incredibly different Western ideas. Like the rest of us, they both have a heart and a mouth. Unlike most of us, their mouths are huge. Oh, I might sell a few thousand books here and there, but these two are big time.

On one hand we have Starhawk who is well-known in the Pagan community for her book *Spiral Dance*. She is known internationally as an activist in what might best be described as the "Echo Feminist Witchcraft Movement".[2] On the other hand, we have Rush Limbaugh, who is well-known in the Pagan community for his support of what many Pagans see as the far-right agenda. Although he might not have the trappings that we normally associate with social activism, he gets his message across loud and clear.

The Neo-Pagan movement has had a long history of social activism, and Starhawk has led that path on many occasions. So active is she in the realm of social reform that I have spoken to many Pagan event organizers who won't ask her to speak because they are afraid she will have to cancel because of yet another arrest. Starhawk, I commend you and anyone with your spirit, but are your tactics actually achieving social reform or just giving Rush Limbaugh one more "Environmental Wacko"[3] to poke fun at?

This is not to say that it is not absolutely necessary to take an active role in the protection of Mother Earth, but the laws of science, nature, and of magick agree that for every action there is an equal and opposite reaction. This is why the Pagan way of science, nature, and magick is more of nurturing a single ember into a fire, rather than tossing a match into a can of gasoline. In the first case, your kith and kin will huddle for warmth. In the later, if they are smart, they will run for their lives.

This is probably why, in response to the protest of the World Economic Summit in New York (held February 1–3, 2002, shortly after September 11, 2001), *The Village Voice*, which is normally very supportive of Starhawk's efforts, printed an article that Starhawk described as "...straight out of the police propaganda factory." In essence, *The Village Voice* ran for its life when they saw that match headed for the can of gasoline. Whatever the message of that protest was, it was lost in the general consensus that, after September 11th, the City of New York deserved a break.

Lost, too, was the message behind the protests against the World Trade Organization (WTO) on the other side of the United States. In a book titled *Globalize This!* (edited by Kevin Danaher and Roger Burbach), a collection of writings by different authors tells the story of the battle against the WTO. Section I, Part II, "How We Really Shut Down the WTO," is credited to Starhawk.

Yes, Starhawk and associates did more or less shut down the WTO's meeting, but what was really accomplished? If you were to randomly ask people on the street what they thought of the WTO, most of them would think you are talking about the WWE. Most people have never heard of the WTO, much less of Starhawk's objections to it. On the other hand, most people have heard about the riots in Seattle, which just about shut down the city.

Again, I must say that I adore Starhawk. I do not always agree with her, but I adore her, nonetheless, for her never-ending battle to speak what she believes. Now for the statement that will probably end my career as a Pagan author: I also adore Rush Limbaugh. I do not always agree with him either, but I adore him as well, for his never-ending battle to speak what he believes.

When it comes to causing change, the problem with both of these folks is that they were both born with the same birth defect that my mother tells me I am afflicted with: the tendency to overfocus on one's own opinion, complicated with a complete and total lack of tact. Maybe they, too, are Leos. As a result, the people who listen to them are usually people who already agree with them. What change is there in that? Backing people into a wall is not the way to get a point across, because that is where they will resist the most. Clearly, this is not the best way to win friends and influence people:

> "Listen first. Give your opponents a chance to talk. Let them finish. Do not resist, defend or debate. This only raises barriers. Try to build bridges of understanding. Don't build higher barriers of misunderstanding."
>
> —From *Bits and Pieces*, published by the Economic Press (Fairfield, NJ) as quoted from *How to Win Friends & Influence People*, Revised Edition, by Dale Carnegie (Pocket Books, 1981)

Neither is it the way to win a war:

> "In a desperate situation they fear nothing; when there is no way out they stand firm."
>
> —From *The Art of War* by Sun Tzu, translated by Samuel Griffith (Oxford University Press, 1971)

And it most certainly is not the way of Wicca:

> "Soft of eye and light of touch—speak little, listen much."
>
> —From Rede of the Wiccae[4]

Finding Common Ground

The emulsifier that can bring Starhawk to dinner at the Limbaughs' is common ground. Trust me on this one, I know it is hard to hold your tongue when someone says something incredibly offensive, but sometimes that is exactly what it takes to find common ground. Let's look at Rush and Starhawk.

One might say women should be allowed to work as equals. The other might say women should have the right to remain at home and tend her children. Aren't both essentially telling us that women should have the right to decide for themselves what best their role is?

One might argue that English should be our national language. The other might argue that this would put non-English-speaking people at a disadvantage. Aren't both essentially telling us that they want to further communications?

One might argue that the logging industry should be abolished because it cuts down trees. The other might argue that the logging industry has planted more trees than it has cut down. Are they not both demonstrating a concern for the environment?

And what about the war in the Middle East? Surely both Rush and Starhawk would not want their children to die in such a conflict. On this, I am reminded of an English professor and his wild story that took place during the Vietnam War. Although I cannot substantiate his claim, he once told my class that he helped write the song "I Feel Like I'm Fixing to Die."

I argued that it was written by Country Joe. He said it was written by Country Joe and the Fish (with emphases on "the Fish"). I argued that my professor wasn't Country Joe. He agreed, claiming he was the Fish. I didn't believe him then, and I am not sure if I believe him now, but for some reason we spent the rest of the hour listening to his love story that reportedly took place during the Vietnam War. Like mythology, having basis in fact or fiction does not change a story's ability to stress a point.

As I am sure you can imagine, the professor was an anti-war activist. While protesting outside of the Peace Talks in Paris, he met a beautiful young woman who worked in a political capacity for North Vietnam. They fell in love. Why not? After all, they both agreed that the war should end. They found common ground. As if the relationship was not ill fated enough, fortune handed it a devastating blow: His love was forced to become a soldier by the North Vietnamese government.

How, you might ask, could someone so opposed to the war love someone who fought in it, especially when she fought against troops of his very country? Because no matter what side of a war one is on, the common goal is an end to the war. Be you soldier or protestor, love is the law.

So What Might We Have in Common With Other World Religions?

The commonalties of religion are more in the heart than in the words:

Question: Who do you worship?

Answer: The same God as you. I just view him differently.

Ah, but what about the Lady? Here is an excellent example of what I mean by heart mattering more than words. Just as we all have different views of our Lord and Lady, different people give that Creator differing names. Some say God, some say the union of Lord and Lady. But when you get to the heart of it, the Creator is the same.

Question: What is all this about magick and spells?

Answer: Spells are like prayers. Magick is when prayers are answered.

In a very real way, our spells are prayers. The difference between them is much the same as the differing views of the Creator. Where other religions see their prayers going to their God, we see our spells cast to the creative forces that we consider the Creator (remember, thou art God and Goddess). We just use a few more props.

Remember, almost every world religion has come up with at least one commonality: The Golden Rule.

Maybe It Will Work

Consider the online community of computer programmers (yet another circle I belong to):

> There is a programming language called Visual Basic developed by Microsoft. There is a Website (domain name) not owned by Microsoft by the name of *www.visualbasic.com*. On the Website, the owner is clear in disclaiming any connection to Microsoft, and it has become a valuable asset to those of us who frequent it. In much the same way, my site at *www.neopagan.com* and Issac Bonewits' site *www.neopagen.net* respect each other by posting a notice on our front page whenever the other is on the radio, TV, or in other way promoting his site.

Here we see an example of how even a giant corporate entity has embraced our law and how two Pagan authors have done much the same. And yet in the same realm, we continue to fail to do the same.

Maybe It Won't work

Sometime earlier this year, I purchased the Web domain *witchesvoice.com*. Knowing that someone else owned the domain *witchesvoice.org*, I wrote them an e-mail to politely explain that I had purchased the domain and didn't see much of a conflict because of that all important "dot-com" indicating a commercial intent. Their domain was dot-org, indicating their organizational intent.

Instead of hearing concerns in a reply e-mail, I heard threats and demands from their lawyer. Instead of nurturing those embers, they threw a match in my figurative can of gasoline. My knee-jerk reaction: I purchased the domain *witchesvoice.net* and began the long process of creating the Witches Farce, a parody site designed to offer critical commentary on the Pagan community with a flavor of satire. How will it end? Well, time will tell, but I hope we all get a good chuckle.

At Least We Can Say We Tried

In closing this chapter, I stumbled upon a very interesting synchronicity. I read Sun Tzu's *The Art of War* and Dale Carnegie's *How to Win Friends & Influence People*, both because they were recommended to me by friends. After reading both, I returned the friends' favor by recommending the opposite book back to each. You see, upon reading each, I was left with a tremendous sense of imbalance much like I am when I think of either the Witch War of 1971 or the books by the Farrars that started to be printed in 1981. What makes this very interesting is that the version of *The Art of War* that I stumbled upon was published in 1971, and the version of *How to Win Friends & Influence People* was published in 1981. I don't see any great message in this synchronicity, but neither do I believe in coincidence.

I don't know if either of those friends will take my advice, read the other book, and find balance, but at least I can say I tried. For the most part, that is all anyone can do. We can try to change the macrocosm of our world by addressing the microcosm of human relationships in our everyday life. If it doesn't work, well at least we tried.

A Final Word

In Chapter 1, I told you that I once heard the words of the Goddess as plain as one can hear the words of a lover incarnate. Upon hearing those words, I started my search for her embrace. I have yet to find her, so here I cast my greatest aspiration to the universe with the words of the greatest storyteller the universe has ever known:

> "O speak again, bright angel, for thou art
> As glorious to this night, being o'er my head,
> As is a winged messenger of heaven
> Unto the white upturned wond'ring eyes
> Of mortals that fall back to gaze on him
> When he bestrides the lazy puffing clouds
> And sails upon the bosom of the air."
>
> —William Shakespeare, *Romeo and Juliet* 2.1

Thus I end this book with the same quote that it began and the hope that we all find that which our souls demand.

> "The books all talked about love and nature. I didn't see anything wrong with that."
>
> —Denessa Smith, as quoted by
> *The Detroit News*, March 7, 2001

Blessed be and live free,

A.J. Drew

Appendix A

The Origins of the
Wiccan Rede and the
Grandmother's Story

Finding the exact origin of the Wiccan Rede is impossible. It has been in far too many hands prior to its initial publication for us to really be certain. Many attribute its writing to Lady Gwen Thompson, because she submitted it (in one form) to *Green Egg* magazine with the claim that she had received it from her grandmother. *Green Egg* magazine published this poem as the Rede of the Wiccae (see Appendix C).

Three years later, a different work called the Witches Creed was published by Doreen Valiente (see Appendix B). This might be the cause for the confusion, as Valiente is often cited as the author of the Wiccan Rede and because the titles are similar. On the other hand, it is entirely possible that the Wiccan Rede actually was written by Doreen Valiente and not published.

So, it was (in one form) submitted to *Green Egg* magazine by Thompson with one title. Three years later Doreen Valiente published something with different content, but a similar title. Neither was titled the Wiccan Rede. Things just can't be that easy. Instead, there is now a poem that is repeatedly titled the Wiccan Rede. (See Appendix D.)

On the other hand, we have the grandmother story. Per Alex Sanders, the Alexandrian tradition was passed to him from his Grandmother. She, being dead, couldn't argue the issue.

And yet, even though the Alexandrian tradition was reportedly handed from grandmother to grandson, a great deal of the tradition looks almost word for word like what Doreen Valiente wrote for the Gardnerian tradition. I have no overwhelming reason to doubt that Lady Gwen Thompson's grandmother gave her the poem that she submitted to *Green Egg* magazine, but it does look a great deal like yet another "grandmother story."

With the poem set aside, this is what we can find of the Rede itself:

> "An these eight words the Wiccan Rede fulfill, An ye harm none do as ye will."

I think the idea is definitely based contemporarily in Aleister Crowley's Law of Thelema, but I do not for a moment think that Thelema was one of Crowley's original ideas.

François Rabelais (1494–1553)

In his book *Gargantua* (1532), François Rabelais describes a perfect Utopia by the name of the "Abbey of Theleme," whose law is "Do as you wish."

Pierre Louÿs (1870–1925)

In his novel *Les Aventures du Roi Pausole* (aka *The Adventures of King Pausole*), Pierre Louÿs describes how King Pausole makes an ancient book of customs much more understandable by distilling its meaning into, "Do no wrong to thy neighbor. Observing this, do as thou pleaseth." Gardner himself cites this story in his book *The Meaning of Witchcraft*.

Aleister Crowley (1875–1947)

No one knows the first time Aleister Crowley wrote the Law of Thelema. A safe bet is in the *Book of the Law* (Liber Al vel Legis, first issued privately by the Ordo Templi Orientis [O.T.O.] 1938):

> "Do what thou wilt shall be the whole of the Law."

Gerald B. Gardner (1884–1964)

In his book *The Meaning of Witchcraft* (1959), Gerald Gardner writes and tells us that Witches "are inclined to the morality of the legendary Good King Pausol: 'Do what you like so long as you harm no one.'"

The Witches Creed
By Doreen Valiente

1   Hear now the words of the witches,
2   The secrets we hid in the night,
3   When dark was our destiny's pathway,
4   That now we bring forth into the light.
5   Mysterious water and fire,
6   The earth and the wide-ranging air.
7   By hidden quintessence we know them,
8   And will and keep silent and dare.

9   The birth and rebirth of all nature,
10   The passing of winter and spring,
11   We share with the life universal,
12   Rejoice in the magickal ring.
13   Four times in the year the Great Sabbat Returns,
14   And the witches are seen,
15   At Lammas and Candlemass dancing,
16   On May Even and old Hallowe'en.

17   When day-time and night-time are equal,
18   When sun is at greatest and least,
19   The four Lesser Sabbats are summoned,
20   Again witches gather in feast.

21   Thirteen silver moons in a year are,
22   Thirteen is the coven's array,
23   Thirteen times at esbat make merry,
24   For each golden year and a day.

25   The power was passed down the ages,
26   Each time between woman and man,
27   Each century unto the other,
28   Ere time and the ages began.

29   When drawn is the magickal circle,
30   By sword or athame or power,
31   Its compass between the two worlds lies,
32   In Land of the Shades for that hour.
33   This world has no right then to know it,
34   And world of beyond will tell naught,
35   The oldest of Gods are invoked there,
36   The Great Work of magick is wrought.

37   For two are the mystical pillars,
38   That stand at the gate of the shrine,
39   And two are the powers of nature,
40   The forms and the forces divine.

41   The dark and the light in succession,
42   The opposites each unto each,
43   Shown forth as a God and a Goddess:
44   Of this did our ancestors teach.

45   By night he's the wild wind's rider,
46   The Horn'd One, the Lord of the Shades.
47   By day he's the King of the Woodland,
48   The dweller in green forest glades.

49   She is youthful and old as she pleases,
50   She sails the torn clouds in her barque,
51   The bright silver Lady of midnight,
52   The crone who weaves spells in the dark.

53   The master and mistress of magick,
54   They dwell in the deeps of the mind,
55   Immortal and ever-renewing,
56   With power to free or to bind.

57   So drink the good wine to the old Gods,
58   And dance and make love in their praise,
59   Till Elphame's* fair land shall receive us,
60   In peace at the end of our days.

61   And Do What You Will be the challenge,
62   So be it in love that harms none,
63   For this is the only commandment.
64   By magick of old be it done!

*Note: In the Celtic Pantheon, Queen Elphame is the Goddess of Death and rebirth.

Appendix C

Rede of the Wiccae

Submitted to *Green Egg Magazine* by Lady Gwen Thompson. First published in Vol. III, No. 69 (Ostara, 1975). Thompson claimed she received the poem from her grandmother, Adriana Porter.

1. Bide the Wiccan laws ye must in perfect love and perfect trust.
2. Live and let live—fairly take and fairly give.
3. Cast the Circle thrice about to keep all evil spirits out.
4. To bind the spell every time, let the spell be spake in rhyme.
5. Soft of eye and light of touch—speak little, listen much.
6. Deosil go by the waxing Moon—sing and dance the Wiccan rune.
7. Widdershins go when the Moon doth wane, and the Werewolf howls by the dread Wolfsbane.
8. When the Lady's moon is new, kiss the hand to her times two.
9. When the Moon rides at her peak, then your heart's desire seek.

10   Heed the Northwind's mighty gale—lock the door and drop the sail.

11   When the wind comes from the South, love will kiss thee on the mouth.

12   When the wind blows from the East, expect the new and set the feast.

13   When the West wind blows o'er thee, departed spirits restless be.

14   Nine woods in the Cauldron go—burn them quick and burn them slow.

15   Elder be ye Lady's tree—burn it not or cursed ye'll be.

16   When the Wheel begins to turn—let the Beltane fires burn.

17   When the Wheel has turned a Yule, light the Log and let Pan rule.

18   Heed ye flower, bush and tree—by the Lady blessed be.

19   Where the rippling waters go, cast a stone an truth ye'll know.

20   When ye have need, hearken not to other's greed.

21   With the fool no season spend or be counted as his friend.

22   Merry meet an merry part—bright the cheeks an warm the heart.

23   Mind the Threefold Law ye should—three times bad and three times good.

24   When misfortune is enow, wear the blue star on thy brow.

25   True in love ever be unless thy lover's false to thee.

26   Eight words the Wiccan Rede fulfill—an it harm none, do what ye will.

Appendix D

The Wiccan Rede

I have seen the poem of the Wiccan Rede in many slightly different formats and cited to many different authors. This is as it appears in my Book of Shadows (better called a scrapbook of shadows). Although faded, the words are as I hand-copied them back in 1979 from the book of one who claimed to be a student of Mercedes Lacky. I have not had contact with Mercedes since that time in my youth, so I cannot confirm the source. It is entirely possible that the woman I met simply combined the Rede of the Wiccae (Appendix C) with her own words. But I have seen the Rede quoted word for word as it is presented here in the hands of many people she could not have met. Most notably, in the hands of a close friend whom I met in Germany (1984). Although I would have no problem believing it could have migrated that fast today, this was pre-Internet migration of ideas from someone in South Bend, Indiana, to someone in Frankfurt, West Germany.

Ultimately, I can't imagine the poem that appeared in *Green Egg* magazine in 1975 could have trickled into such widespread and reportedly ancient lore in just the four years prior to my reading it for the first time in a handwritten journal. Instead, I feel that while we might be able to discover its first printing, the true origin of the Wiccan Rede will never be discovered.

1   Bide the Wiccan laws ye must, in perfect love and perfect trust.

2   Ye must live and let to live, fairly take and fairly give.

3   Throw the circle thrice about, to keep unwelcome spirits out.

4   To bind ye spell every time, let ye spell be spake in rhyme.

5   Soft of eye, light of touch, speak ye little, listen much.

6   Deosil go by the waxing moon, chanting out the Witches' Rune.

7   Widdershins go by the waning moon, chanting out a baneful tune.

8   When the Lady's moon is new, kiss the hand to her, times two.

9   When the moon rides at her peak, then your heart's desire seek.

10 Heed the North wind's mighty gale, lock the door and trim the sail.

11 When the wind comes from the South, love will kiss thee on the mouth.

12 When the wind blows from the West, departed souls will have no rest.

13 When the wind blows from the East, expect the new and set the feast.

14 Nine woods in the cauldron go, burn them fast and burn them slow.

15 But elder be the Lady's tree, burn it not or cursed you'll be.

16 When the Wheel begins to turn, let the Beltane fires burn.

17 When the Wheel has turned to Yule, light the log, let the Horned One rule.

18 Heed ye Flower, Bush and Tree, by the Lady, blessed be.

19 Where the rippling waters go, cast a stone and truth you'll know.

20 When ye have a true need, hearken not to others' greed.

21 Never a season with a fool shall ye spend, lest be counted as his friend.

22 Merry meet and merry part, bright the cheeks and warm the heart.

23 Less in thy own defense it be, always mind the rule of three.

24 When misfortune is enow, wear the blue star on thy brow.

25 True in Love ever be, lest thy lover's false to thee.

26 These eight words the Wiccan Rede fulfill: An ye harm none, do as ye will.

Appendix E

The Oath of Hippocrates

I swear by Apollo the physician, and Æsculapius, and Hygeia, and Panacea, and all the gods and goddesses, that according to my ability and judgment, I will keep this oath and its stipulations—to reckon him who taught me this art equally dear to me as my parents, to share my substance with him, and to relieve his necessities if required; to look upon his offspring in the same footing as my own brothers, and to teach them this art if they shall wish to learn it, without fee or stipulation, and that by precept, lecture, and every other mode of instruction, I will impart a knowledge of the art to my own sons, and those of my teachers, and to disciples bound by a stipulation and oath according to the law of medicine, but to none other.

I will follow that system of regimen which, according to my ability and judgment, I consider for the benefit of my patients, and abstain from whatever is deleterious and mischievous. I will give no deadly medicine to anyone if asked, nor suggest any such counsel; and in like manner I will not give to a woman a pessary to produce abortion. With purity and holiness I will pass my life and practice my art. I will not cut persons laboring under the stone, but will leave this to be done by men who are practitioners of this work. Into whatever houses I enter, I will go into them for the benefit of the sick, and will abstain from every voluntary act of mischief and corruption; and, further, from the seduction of females or males, of freemen and slaves. Whatever, in connection with my professional practice, or not in connection with it, I see or hear, in the life of men, which ought not to be spoken of abroad, I will not divulge, as reckoning that all such should be kept secret.

While I continue to keep this Oath unviolated, may it be granted to me to enjoy life and the practice of this art, respected by all men, in all time. But should I trespass and violate this Oath, may the reverse be my lot.

Chapter Notes

Chapter 1

[1] Rede of the Wiccae. Submitted to *Green Egg* magazine by Lady Gwen Thompson. First published in Vol. III. No. 69 (Ostara, 1975). Thompson claimed she received the poem from her grandmother, Adriana Porter. See Appendix C.

[2] The Law of Thelema. Conceptual origins unclear. See Appendix A.

[3] Demography and Roman Society by Professor Tim G. Parkins (Johns Hopkins UP, 1992).

Chapter 2

[1] From *Witchcraft: Ancient & Modern* by Raymond Buckland (HC Publishers, 1970). This book has been reprinted. In its reprint, several lines may have changed. I have quoted the first edition from my own personal library.

[2] From *Witchcraft from the Inside* by Raymond Buckland (Llewellyn Publications, 1971).

Chapter 5

[1] It's really a great deal more than a chat network, but I won't bore you with the details here. Better you find them at *www.pagannation.com*.

[2] Recently, I have noticed some Wiccans have opted for the term Mistress rather than Maiden. Thus they would refer to

the three stages of Goddess as Mistress, Mother, and Crone. I am inclined to think that this does serve well to equal the field between Lord and Lady in their association with each other. Mistress (a young lady) does tend to go better with Master (a young man). However, it is also clear that the use of these generic titles might lead some to believe the titles denote a dominance of one over the other.

Chapter 6

[1] The Granny Smith apple is very sour and is typically only used for baking pies, and only then with the addition of large amounts of sugar.

[2] Some folks prefer to use earth or rock salt over sea salt. I prefer sea salt because it was separated from water. In so choosing, one is again reminded that we are separated for the sake of union.

[3] I just made that up, but who really knows?

[4] For a more complete explanation, see *Wicca for Men*, which includes diagrams on the casting of the circle in this manner.

[5] Fruit juice can be substituted for wine. It is often the better choice if you do not know for an absolute fact that there are no alcoholics present. As Host and Hostess, it is your duty to insure that your guests are able to partake safely in your rite.

Chapter 7

[1] While it might seem that the third handfasting be better during the winter months, the winter is a time better for reflection than deliberate change.

[2] Bell, book, and candle was originally a reference to the last three things done at the end of some Catholic rites.

Chapter 9

[1] I have not researched the issue of midwife training sufficiently to advise either for or against their use. However, it is my understanding that some states outlaw this practice while others license midwives. I suggest that if you are insistent

upon using a midwife, you do so only where the legal juris-
diction certifies the midwife in a similar manner as a doctor.

[2] The husband stitch is an urban legend that implies all male
doctors deliberately stitch the vagina tighter than it was prior
to childbirth to please the husband. In truth, while this practice may have occurred historically, and even today in rare
circumstances, today's doctors are interested in their
patient's health. Maybe it is some twisted interpretation of
the medical community and its historic connection to the
church (Genesis 3:16).

[3] The pentagram is curiously hard to find in Pagan lore, however it is present time and time again in Christian lore. It
has stood for the five women from the Old Testament, the
five wounds of Christ, and most notably as an Amish symbol to ward off Witches.

Chapter 11

[1] Some cite the Neolithic Revolution as starting as early as
10,000 B.C. (about 12,000 years ago), however the majority
cite the start between 6500 and 7000 B.C. (8,500 to 9,000 years
ago).

[2] The term "Echo Feminist Witchcraft Movement" is sometimes shortened to "Echo Feminist Movement" to better
suit the context in which it is used.

[3] The term "Environmental Wacko" is used so often by Rush
Limbaugh that many think he coined it.

[4] This is line 5 of the Rede of the Wiccae as published in
Green Egg magazine, Volume III, No. 69 (Ostara, 1975). It
is interesting to note that it is not contained in Doreen
Valiente's The Witches Creed, as first published in her book
Witchcraft for Tomorrow (Hale, London 1978).

Bibliography

Books

Buckland, Raymond. *Buckland's Complete Book of Witchcraft*. St Paul, Minn.: Llewellyn Worldwide, 1986.

——. *Witchcraft: Ancient and Modern*. New York: HC Publishers, 1970.

——. *Witchcraft from the Inside*. St Paul, Minn.: Llewellyn Worldwide, 1971.

Carnegie, Dale. *How to Win Friends & Influence People*. New York: Pocket Books, 1981.

Cunningham, Scott. *Wicca: A Guide for the Solitary Practitioner*. St Paul, Minn.: Llewellyn Worldwide, 1988.

Farrar, Janet and Steward. *The Witches Goddess*. Custer, Wash.: Phoenix, 1987.

Farrar, Steward. *What Witches Do*. Custer, Wash.: Phoenix, 1995.

Grimassi, Raven. *Encyclopedia of Wicca and Witchcraft*. St Paul, Minn.: Llewellyn Worldwide, 2000.

Judith, Anodea. *The Truth About Neo-Paganism*. St. Paul, Minn.: Llewellyn Worldwide, 1994.

Knight, Sirona. *Love, Sex, and Magick*. Secaucus, N.J.: Citadel, 1999.

Leland, Charles. *Aradia*. Buckland Museum, New York, 1968.

McArthur, Margie. *Wiccacraft for Families*. Custer, Wash.: Phoenix, 1994.

Morrison, Dorothy. *Enchantments of the Heart*. Franklin Lakes, N.J.: New Page Books, 2002.

Ravenwolf, Silver. *To Ride a Silver Broomstick*. St. Paul, Minn.: Llewellyn Worldwide, 1993.

Reed, Ellen Cannon. *The Heart of Wicca*. York Beach, Maine: Weiser, 2000.

Rhea, Lady Maeve. *Handfasted and Heartjoined*. New York: Citadel, 2001.

Shakespeare, William. *Romeo and Juliet*. New York: Oxford, 2000.

Tzu, Sun. *The Art of War*. New York: Oxford, 1971.

Home-spun Newsletters

Martello, Dr. Leo Louis, editor. *The Wicca Newsletter,* Numbers 1–27. Witches International Craft Associates, N.Y., 1970–1973.

———. *Witchcraft Digest Magazine #1.* Witches International Craft Associates, N.Y., 1972.

———. *Witchcraft Digest Magazine #2.* Witches International Craft Associates, N.Y., 1972.

Pentagram: A Witchcraft Review. London: August 1964.

Pentagram: A Witchcraft Review. London, November 1964.

Pentagram: A Witchcraft Review. London, March 1965.

Index

About the Author

A.J. Drew, author of *Wicca Spellcraft for Men* (New Page Books, 2001) *and Wicca for Men*, is the owner of Salem West, one of the largest Neo-Pagan/Wiccan shops in the Midwest. A.J. also hosts the Real Witches Ball, one of the single-largest Pagan gatherings in the United States. He is the founder of *www.neopagan.com*, which was designed to be an online hub for the entire Pagan community.